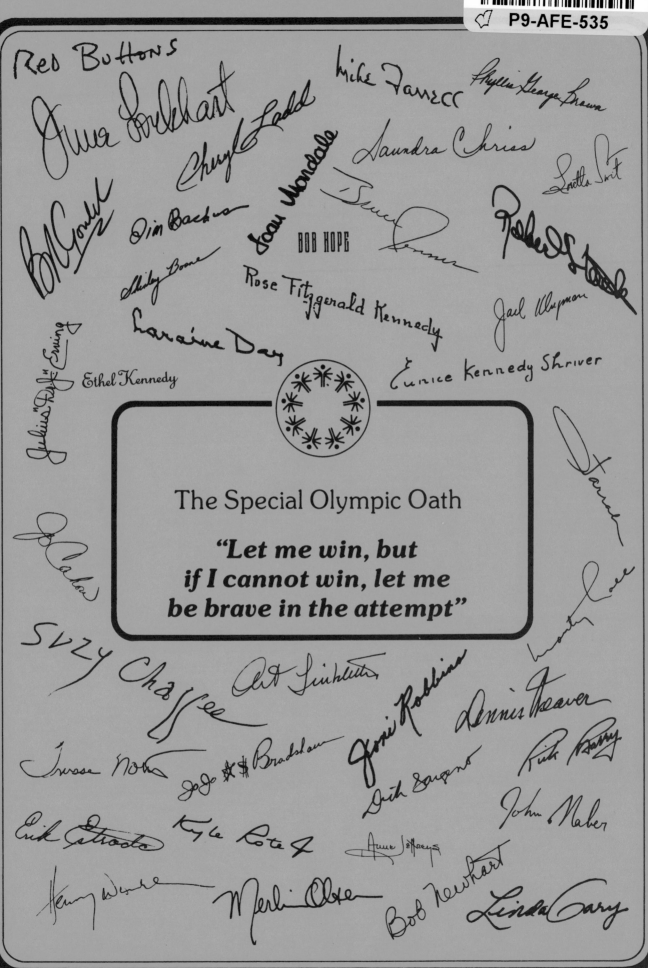

The Special Olympic Oath

"Let me win, but
if I cannot win, let me
be brave in the attempt"

OFFICIAL
SPECIAL OLYMPICS
Celebrity Cook Book

PIPER

East Coast   *Executive Offices*   *West Coast*
NEW YORK CITY   •   BLUE EARTH, MN 56103   •   SAN FRANCISCO

OFFICIAL
SPECIAL OLYMPICS

Celebrity
Cook Book

Foreword by Eunice Kennedy Shriver

by

Kathryn Buursma and Mary Stickney,

Coeditors

Manufactured in the United States of America.

International Standard Book Number: 0-87832-046-6

Library of Congress Catalog Card Number: 79-3044

First Edition, Second Printing

Library of Congress Cataloging–in Publication Data
Main entry under title:

Official Special Olympics celebrity cook book.

    Includes indexes.
    1. Cookery. 2. Special Olympics.
I. Buursma, Kathryn. II. Stickney, Mary.
TX715.0338   641.5   79-3044
ISBN 0-87832-046-6

Audrey Gillen
Illustrator

Composition, typesetting and creative work by **Artistat, Inc.**

Dedication

Special Olympians
throughout the world

Contents

Foreword

Foreword

This Special Olympics Celebrity Cook Book brings together favorite recipes of well known people who are devoted to the mentally retarded.

You will enjoy sampling the dishes, from appetizers through desserts, which these marvelous people have contributed to add variety to your menus and to help Special Olympics.

Our thanks to Kathryn Buursma and Mary Stickney, coeditors, for conceiving and planning this cook book. Kathy and Mary got the idea for this book after attending the 1979 Michigan Winter Special Olympics.

They wondered what the great athletes and other celebrities involved in Special Olympics like to eat best. And so they asked them and found them as generous in sharing their recipes as they are in sharing their time and skills with Special Olympians.

After a delicious meal of Billy Kidd's Rocky Mountain Campfire Trout, Rafer Johnson's Ambrosia and Dr. J's Coca Cola Cake, you might want to thank your favorite celebrity by becoming active in Special Olympics.

There are Special Olympics programs in every state, in every province of Canada and in over thirty countries throughout the world.

Volunteers are needed to teach, to coach, to cheer, to encourage the world's one million Special Olympians. If you would like to join the hundreds of celebrities and the thousands of volunteers who are giving new hope and pride to special Olympians and their families, please write to me:

Eunice Kennedy Shriver
Special Olympics Inc.
1701 K Street N.W.
Washington, D.C. 20006

Thanks and good eating.

Eunice Kennedy Shriver

Eunice Kennedy Shriver
President
Special Olympics, Inc.

ONE

Appetizers and Beverages

Deviled Crab

by Larry Brown

Serve this special crab dish as a hot appetizer before a formal dinner or as a light luncheon or supper dish with a tossed salad. All the flavors go together to enhance the crab.

Serves: 4 to 6
Oven: 450°

Ingredients:

¾ cup milk
1½ cups soft bread crumbs
2 cups flaked cooked crab meat, (2 cans, 6½ oz. each)
5 hard-cooked egg whites, sliced fine

¾ teaspoon salt
¼ teaspoon dry mustard
⅛ teaspoon cayenne pepper
½ cup butter or margarine, melted

Directions:

Combine milk and bread crumbs. Mix. Stir in crab meat and hard-cooked egg whites. Add salt, dry mustard, cayenne pepper and butter to mixture. Mix.

Pour into a buttered 9x9" square pan or individual, lightly buttered shells. Sprinkle with crumbs. Bake in a 450° oven for 15 minutes. Serve hot.

Stuffed Vine Leaves

by Art Buchwald

Greek cuisine has inspired this favorite recipe. The stuffed vine leaves are delicious.

Serves: 10 to 12
Oven: 300°

Ingredients:

Stuffing:
a little olive oil
1 medium onion, sliced
4 oz. ground beef, lean
4 oz. long-grain rice
seasoning
1 tablespoon chopped
   parsley
a little lemon juice

few chopped nuts, mixed
a little tomato paste
30 young vine leaves

Sauce:
1 pint beef stock
1 tablespoon tomato paste
juice of ½ lemon
a little sour cream or yogurt

Directions:

First, prepare the stuffing. Heat the oil, toss the onion, meat and rice in this for approximately 10 minutes, taking care the mixture does not burn. Add enough water to cover, add seasoning, parsley and lemon juice. Simmer gently for 20 minutes until rice is tender. Cool. Add the chopped nuts and tomato paste.

Next, prepare the vine leaves. If using fresh leaves, boil in salted water for about 5 minutes. Drain and spread out flat. Put a little of the stuffing on each leaf and roll firmly. Place at the bottom of oven-proof dish and cover with odd bits of leaves. Arrange a second layer of filled vine leaves if necessary.

Combine beef stock, tomato paste and lemon and pour over stuffed vine leaves. Bake in covered dish for approximately 2 hours at 300°.

If serving hot, lift out stuffed leaves and strain liquid. Reheat, adding the sour cream or yogurt and pour over leaves. If serving cold, allow to stand in the liquid until quite cool and drain well.

Art Buchwald

Remarkable Reds

by Samuel Chew, Jr.

"Serve as a really delightful compliment to red meat . . . at room temperature. It is a consistent crowd pleaser."

Serves: 6 to 8

Ingredients:

6 red bell peppers, sliced
¼ cup olive oil
4 cloves garlic, minced
½ cup freshly grated
    Parmesan cheese

½ cup freshly grated
    Romano cheese

Directions:

Heat oil and garlic in pan. Add sliced peppers and stir fry until they start to burn, "really." When just turning brown, remove from heat and let cool to room temperature.

Sprinkle grated cheeses on top, add salt and pepper to taste.

Samuel Chew, Jr.

Hot Cheese Spread

by Laraine Day

Every cookbook should have a super way to serve bread — a steak lover's favorite meal. This one is great!

Serves: 12
Oven: 450°

Ingredients:

½ cup mayonnaise
1 cup grated Parmesan
   cheese
1 cup shredded Cheddar
   cheese
1 tablespoon chopped
   green onion

salt and pepper to taste
dash of Worcestershire
   sauce
1 small loaf French bread

Directions:

In bowl, combine all ingredients except bread. Spread cheese mixture on slices of French bread and bake at 450° for 5 to 10 minutes. Serve hot.

Laraine Day

"The Green Death"

by Mike Farrell

Mike says, "Enjoy." He should also tell you about the nutritional virtues of all the ingredients. Maybe it will get you into health food!

Yield: 1 to 1½ quarts

Ingredients:

fruit juice of choice
(preferably apple),
about 1 quart
½ papaya
1 Delicious apple, pared
and cored
8 almonds, ground
4 teaspoons chia, ground
3 teaspoons sesame seeds,
ground
¾ cup sunflower seeds,
ground
¾ cup pumpkin seeds,
ground

1 tablespoon yeast powder
1 tablespoon lecithin
powder
1 tablespoon protein
powder
1 tablespoon bee pollen
2 teaspoons sesame oil
4 teaspoons liquid
chlorophyll
4 tablespoons aloe vera
(Aloe Vera Gel)

Directions:

Put ingredients in blender. Blend to consistency of your choice by regulating the amount of juice.

Mike Farrell

Discus Turkey Hors d'Oeuvres

by Fortune Gordien

Fresh ground turkey combines with onion and cheese and bakes into a delicious hot hors d'oeuvres.

Serves: 4
Oven: 350°

Ingredients:

½ cup ground turkey, uncooked

¾ cup shredded Cheddar cheese

1 teaspoon onion juice or onion flakes

1 egg

¼ cup salted cracker crumbs, finely crushed

Directions:

Combine turkey, cheese, onion and egg. Mix well. Form mixture into 12 to 14 miniature discus. Coat each discus with the cracker crumbs; place on greased cookie sheet. Bake at 350° for 30 minutes. Serve hot or cold.

Fortune Gordien

SPECIAL OLYMPICS BOOSTER

Fruit Zinger

by Valerie Harper

A marvelous drink for meal skippers — extra nutrition, energy and "get up and go" for anyone.

Yield: approx. 1 quart

Ingredients:

2 cups papaya juice
1 fresh papaya
2 fresh peaches
2 plums or apricots
1 pint low fat yogurt, fruit
    flavor (peach or
    pineapple)

1 tablespoon lecithin
1 tablespoon wheatgerm
1 teaspoon honey (pure
    organic)

Directions:

Put contents in a blender and blend away! To thin out, add spring water.

Valerie Harper

SPECIAL OLYMPICS VOLUNTEER

Hot Crab Dip

by Lee Roy Jordan

Having a special crowd over for dinner? Start the evening with this delicious crab dip with a curry note.

Yield: About 4 cups

Ingredients:

2 cartons (8 oz. ea.) sour cream
1 pkg. (8 oz.) cream cheese
1 cup mayonnaise
2 teaspoons lemon juice

1½ teaspoons salt
1 tablespoon Accent
1 tablespoon curry powder
1 lb. lump crabmeat

Directions:

Mix all ingredients except crab until smooth in double boiler. Add crab and mix well. Heat, but do not boil. Serve with toast points.

Lee Roy Jordan

Salmon Ball

by Sarah Kennedy

The only way you can describe this appetizer is "yummy and elegant."

Serves: 15 to 20

Ingredients:

2 cups canned salmon
3½ tablespoons lemon
    juice
4 tablespoons grated onion
2 teaspoons horseradish
salt and pepper to taste
1 pkg. (8 oz.) cream cheese,
    softened

1 pkg. (3 oz.) pecans, finely
    chopped
3 tablespoons finely
    chopped fresh parsley
assorted crackers

Directions:

Drain and flake salmon, remove skin and bones. Combine the salmon, lemon juice, onion, horseradish, salt and pepper with cream cheese. Mix well.

Shape into ball. Roll in pecans and parsley. Wrap in foil and refrigerate until serving time. Can be made several days ahead. Can be frozen. Serve with crackers.

Sarah Kennedy

Delicious Ham Roll-Ups

by George Sappenfield

Tortillas are filled with ham, cheese and chilies; then topped with sauce and more cheese — Um Good!

Serves: 12
Oven: 350°

Ingredients:

12 flour tortillas
12 slices of ham
12 slices Monterey Jack
    cheese
1 can (4 oz.) green chilies,
    diced
¾ lb. shredded Cheddar
    cheese

Basic White Sauce:

½ cup flour
½ cup butter
1 quart milk
1 teaspoon salt
¼ teaspoon pepper

Directions:

Melt butter in saucepan. Sprinkle in flour, salt and pepper, stirring constantly. Gradually stir in milk.

Put slice of ham, cheese and some chilies on each tortilla and roll up. Place folded side down in two 9x13″ baking dishes. Pour white sauce over tortillas. Sprinkle with cheese. Bake at 350° for 45 minutes.

George Sappenfield

21

Avocado Green Chili Dip

by Dick Sargent

"This is also great as a baked potato topping or mixed into scrambled eggs!"

Yield: 2 cups

Ingredients:

1 can (4 oz.) green chilies, diced
1 large avocado, diced
1 cup sour cream

1 teaspoon salt or 1 to 2 tablespoons lemon juice

Directions:

Mix together chilies, avocado, sour cream and salt. Chill. Serve with taco or potato chips.

Dick Sargent

Sugarless Shake

by Barbara Sigel

"The drink is great when you're in a hurry and very good for you. It tastes so de-lish that you don't crave fattening goodies."

Serves: 1 to 2

Ingredients:

1 pkg. non-fat chocolate flavored milk or 1 pkg. "Alba" chocolate non-fat dry milk

¾ cup ice water
1 egg
3 ice cubes

Directions:

In a blender, mix the powdered milk and water. Add egg. Add one ice cube at a time, continuing to blend. (If you want to use skim milk, add ¼ tablespoon cinnamon and 2 pkgs. of Sweet 'n Low.)

Strawberry Delight

A drink for anytime! A calorie watcher's meal or a nutritious, delicious snack.

Serves: 1 to 2

Ingredients:

⅓ cup skim milk powder or one envelope "Alba" non-fat dry milk
1 cup ice water

1 egg
½ cup strawberries
2 pkgs. Sweet 'n Low
3 ice cubes

Directions:

In a blender, mix the powdered milk and water. Add egg. Add strawberries and Sweet 'n Low and blend. Add one ice cube at a time, continuing to blend.

Barbara Sigel

Stuffed Cabbage Rolls

by Barbara Walters

Cabbage rolls are a favorite of restaurant patrons. This very special recipe is worth the extra time in the kitchen. They refrigerate and freeze beautifully.

Serves: 14
Oven: 375°

Ingredients:

3 lbs. lean ground chuck
2 teaspoons salt
¾ teaspoon pepper
2 teaspoons celery salt
½ cup catsup
2 eggs
½ cup crushed unsalted crackers

2 heads (2 lb. size) green cabbage
6 quarts boiling water
3 cups chopped onion
2 bottles (12 oz. ea.) chili sauce
1 jar (12 oz.) grape jelly

Directions:

In large bowl, combine chuck, salt, pepper, celery salt, catsup, eggs, and crushed crackers. Mix with hands just until mixture is well combined.

Cut out and discard hard center core of cabbage. Place cabbage in large kettle. Pour boiling water over it; let stand until leaves are flexible and can be removed easily from the head — about 5 minutes. (If necessary, return cabbage to hot water to soften inner leaves.)

Using a ¼ cup measure, scoop up a scant ¼ cup meat mixture. With hands, form into rolls, 3″ long and 1″ wide, making about 28 rolls in all.

Place each meat roll on a drained cabbage leaf; fold top of leaf over meat, then fold sides, and roll up into an oblong. Continue rolling remaining meat rolls and cabbage leaves.

CONTINUED —

Stuffed Cabbage Rolls

by Barbara Walters

In bottom of lightly greased 12x11½x2¼″ roasting pan, spread chopped onion evenly. Arrange cabbage rolls in neat rows on top of onion.

In 2 quart saucepan, combine chili sauce and grape jelly with ¼ cup water; heat over medium heat, stirring to melt jelly. Pour over cabbage rolls.

Cover pan tightly with foil. Bake 2 hours. Remove foil; brush rolls with sauce; bake, uncovered, 40 minutes longer, or until sauce is thick and syrupy and cabbage rolls are glazed. Serve with sauce spooned over rolls.

Barbara Walters

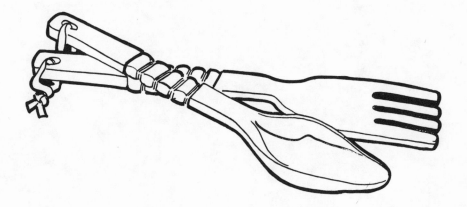

TWO

Baked Specialties

Persimmon Cake

by Lucille Ball

A special fruit, persimmon, bakes up into a delicious cake delicately flavored with spices.

Yield: 2 large loaves or
4 small loaves
Oven: 300°

Ingredients:

2 cups sugar
3 tablespoons butter or
    margarine
2 cups persimmon pulp
2 cups walnuts, chopped
1 cup seedless raisins
1 cup dates, cut fine
rind of one orange, grated
1 cup milk

4 cups cake flour, sifted
2 teaspoons cinnamon
½ teaspoon cloves
½ teaspoon allspice
½ teaspoon nutmeg
4 teaspoons soda
3 teaspoons baking powder
2 teaspoons vanilla extract

Directions:

Cream together sugar and butter. Add remaining ingredients and mix well.

Bake in 2 greased large loaf tins or 4 small ones for 1½ hours at 300°.

Lucy

Italian Sweet Pie

by Ron Carey

A very special "Old World" Italian pie; delicious fruit filling and "melt in the mouth" pastry.

Serves: 10 to 12
Oven: 350°

PASTRY DOUGH

Ingredients:

1¼ cups flour
2 egg yolks
4 tablespoons milk

½ cup powdered sugar
1 teaspoon vanilla
½ cup butter or margarine

Directions:

Sift flour. Add softened butter and blend with fork. Add sugar, vanilla, milk and egg yolks to mixture. Shape into a ball and wrap in plastic wrap. Put in refrigerator for one hour.

Line lightly floured 10″ pie pan with pastry dough. Reserve some for lattice strips. Pour sweet pie mixture into pastry. Make lattice top.

Bake for 1 hour at 350°. After one hour leave in oven with door open for 20 minutes to cool slightly.

FILLING

Ingredients:

2 lbs. ricotta cheese, drained
1½ cups sugar
4 egg yolks
1½ cups cooked wheat (can be purchased at Italian Delicacy store)
1 cup boiled milk, cooled

½ cup combination of chopped citron, chopped orange peel and chopped lemon peel
1 tablespoon vanilla
dash of cinnamon
4 egg whites, stiffly beaten

Directions:

Cream ricotta and sugar. Add egg yolks one at a time. Add wheat and milk and mix together. Add fruit, vanilla and cinnamon. Fold in beaten egg whites.

Ron Carey

Oatmeal Lace Cookies

by Joanna Carson

A marvelous cookie that tastes like caramel and oats. Family and friends will love them.

Yield: approx. 40
Oven: 350°

Ingredients:

½ cup butter
1 cup brown sugar, firmly
    packed

1½ cups quick oats
1 egg, unbeaten
½ teaspoon vanilla

Directions:

Melt butter in the top of a double boiler over gently boiling water. Add the sugar and oats; cook until well blended, stirring occasionally. It takes about 5 minutes. Remove and cool.

Add egg and vanilla; mix thoroughly. Line a cookie sheet with K.V.P. silicone parchment or grease it. Drop by teaspoonful about 2″ apart. You can get 12 cookies on the sheet but they brown better with 8 at a time.

Bake in a moderate oven 350° to 375° for about 12 minutes or until golden brown. *Cool for 2 minutes.* Gently remove from sheet. Cool on cake rack. Don't stack them until they are cool.

Joanna Carson

Fresh Apple Cake

by Samuel Clayton

A spicy fresh apple cake that boasts a buttery topping which soaks into the warm cake.

Serves: 8 to 10
Oven: 350°

CAKE

Ingredients:

½ cup butter or margarine
1 cup sugar
1 egg
1 cup flour
1 teaspoon baking soda
½ teaspoon nutmeg

½ teaspoon cinnamon
¼ teaspoon salt
2 cups unpeeled apples, chopped
¾ cup raisins and/or nutmeats

Directions:

Blend together butter, sugar and egg. Beat until fluffy. Add flour, baking soda, nutmeg, cinnamon and salt. Stir in apples, raisins and/or nutmeats. Bake in a greased 8 x 8 x 2″ pan or 10″ pie plate, at 350° for 35 to 40 minutes.

TOPPING

Ingredients:

¼ cup evaporated milk
¼ cup butter or margarine

¼ cup sugar
1 teaspoon vanilla

Directions:

In saucepan, cook milk, butter, sugar and vanilla for approximately 15 minutes until thick.

Important . . . Topping must be spooned onto cake immediately after taken from oven.

Samuel Clayton

31

Monkey Bread

by Bill Cosby

Pieces of rich dough are dipped in butter before they are placed in the baking pan. The bread bakes up crusty and buttery. Serve hot and just tear off the diamonds.

Yields: 1 loaf
(10″ ring)
Oven: 350°

Ingredients:

5 to 5½ cups all purpose flour
2 pkgs. active dry yeast
⅓ cup sugar
1 teaspoon salt
½ cup water

½ cup milk
½ cup butter
3 large eggs
1 cup or more melted butter for dipping

Directions:

In large mixer bowl combine 1½ cups flour, yeast, sugar and salt. In saucepan heat water milk and butter until warm (120° to 130°), butter need not melt. Add to flour mixture. Add eggs. Beat at low speed until moistened. Beat at medium speed for 3 minutes.

Add enough remaining flour to make soft dough. Knead on a floured surface for 8 to 10 minutes. Place in a greased bowl turning to grease top. Let rise in a warm place until light and doubled, about 1 hour.

Punch down; turn out on floured board. Roll out ¼″ thick. Cut dough into diamonds (with a cookie cutter) or any shape preferred. Dip each piece into melted butter; arrange in a buttered "monkey pan" (10″ tube). Cover and let rise again until almost doubled, about 1 hour. Bake at 350° for 45 minutes or until browned and done.

Bill Cosby

Lattice Cherry Pie

by Doug DeCinces

Even if you're not related to George Washington, or its not February 22, you'll enjoy this classic cherry pie!

Yield: 9" pie
Oven: 400°

Ingredients:

Filling:

1 can (16 oz.),
    pitted tart cherries,
    drain and reserve
    juice
1 cup sugar
3 tablespoons cornstarch
¼ teaspoon salt
¼ teaspoon cinnamon
½ cup juice from cherries
½ teaspoon vanilla
⅛ teaspoon almond extract

Pastry:

2 cups flour
¾ teaspoon salt
½ cup shortening
½ cup chilled butter cut in
    ¼" bits
5 to 6 tablespoons water
1 egg, separated
1 teaspoon sugar

Directions:

Filling — Combine sugar, cornstarch, salt and cinnamon in medium saucepan. Add juice. Cook over medium heat, stir constantly until thick and begins to boil. Boil one minute.

Remove from heat. Add vanilla and almond extract. Fold in drained cherries — set aside.

Pastry — Mix flour and salt. With pastry blender cut in butter and shortening 'til coarse crumbs. Gradually add water. Stir with fork until moist enough to hold together. Form a ball.

Divide in 2 pieces one slightly larger — form 2 balls, on floured cheesecloth roll large ball into a 11" circle ⅛" thick. Fold in half and then in quarters and gently place in 9" pie plate (glass preferred). Trim overhang to 1". Brush with beaten egg white. Spoon in filling. Set aside.

Roll out other ball in 9" circle ⅛" thick — cut ten ½" strips. Moisten rim of crust with water. Place strips in a lattice work pattern. Trim ends and flute edge. Brush strips only with beaten egg yolk. Sprinkle lightly with teaspoon sugar.

Coca Cola Cake

by Julius "Dr. J." Erving

Coca Cola, a surprise cake ingredient, combines with cocoa and marshmallows for a moist cake topped with a rich and nutty frosting.

Serves: 12
Oven: 350°

CAKE

Ingredients:

½ cup shortening
1 cup butter or margarine
3 tablespoons cocoa
1 cup Coca Cola
2 cups sugar
2 cups flour

½ cup buttermilk
2 eggs, beaten
1 teaspoon baking soda
1 teaspoon vanilla
1½ cups miniature marshmallows

Directions:

In a saucepan, bring shortening, margarine, cocoa and Coca Cola to a boil. In a separate bowl, mix sugar and flour. Add boiled mixture to sugar and flour mixture. In another bowl, mix buttermilk, eggs, baking soda and vanilla. Add marshmallows. Add to chocolate mixture. Pour into a greased spring-form pan or a 9x9" square pan. Bake in a 350° oven for 50 to 60 minutes. Ice while cake is hot.

COCA COLA CAKE FROSTING

Ingredients:

½ cup butter or margarine
3 tablespoons cocoa
6 tablespoons Coca Cola
1 box (1 lb.) powdered sugar

1 teaspoon vanilla
1 cup black walnuts or pecans, chopped

Directions:

In a saucepan, boil margarine, cocoa and Coca Cola. Add powdered sugar, vanilla and nutmeats. Spread on hot cake.

Banana-Bran Muffins

by Nanette Fabray

"A great way to start the day for banana lovers and a great way to use up those over-ripe bananas!"

Yields: 12
Oven: 400°

Ingredients:

1 cup flour
2½ teaspoons baking
    powder
½ teaspoon salt
3 tablespoons sugar
1 cup bran flakes or all-
    bran cereal

1 egg
1 cup milk
¼ cup butter, melted
1 banana, mashed

Directions:

Sift flour with dry ingredients. Stir in bran. Combine egg, milk, melted butter, and add all at once to dry ingredients, mixing only until moistened. Fold in mashed banana.

Fill greased muffin tins ¾ full. Bake at 400° for 20 to 25 minutes.

Nanette Fabray

Favorite Lemon Meringue Pie

by Bob Hope

What could top off a meal in a more refreshing way than Fresh Lemon Meringue pie!

Serves: 6 to 8
Oven: 325°

Ingredients:

9″ baked pie shell
1 cup sugar
3 tablespoons cornstarch
1 cup boiling water
4 egg yolks, reserve 3 egg whites

2 tablespoons butter
¼ cup lemon juice
1 teaspoon grated lemon rind
pinch of salt
2 tablespoons sugar

Directions:

In saucepan, combine sugar and cornstarch. Add water slowly, stirring constantly, until *thick* and smooth. Add slightly beaten egg yolks, butter, lemon juice, lemon rind, and pinch of salt.

Cook 2 to 3 minutes. Pour into 9″ baked shell.

Make meringue with 3 egg whites, gradually adding 2 tablespoons of sugar. Bake at 325° for 15 minutes or until light brown.

BOB HOPE

Potato Chip Cookies

by Anne Jeffreys

A quick and easy nutty Potato Chip Cookie a beginner can make!

Yields: 4 Dozen
Oven: 350°

Ingredients:

1 lb. butter
1½ cups sugar
2 teaspoons vanilla
3½ cups flour

1½ cups potato chips, crushed
2 cups pecans, finely chopped

Directions:

Cream butter, sugar and vanilla until fluffy. Gradually add flour, then chips and pecans. Roll into small balls. Bake at 350° on ungreased cookie sheet for 15 minutes or until golden brown. Drain on paper towel.

Raw Apple Cake by Cheryl Ladd

A simple moist, apple spice cake made even more flavor-ful with coffee

Yield: 13x9″ cake
Oven: 350°

Ingredients:

1 cup shortening
2 cups sugar
2 eggs
2 cups raw apples, pared
    and chopped (not
    "Delicious" apples)
1 cup nutmeats and/or
    raisins (optional)

3 cups flour
2 teaspoons cinnamon
1 teaspoon cloves
2 teaspoons baking soda
1 cup *cold* very strong
    black coffee

Directions:

Cream shortening and sugar. Add eggs, and chopped apples. Add nutmeats and/or raisins. Sift together, flour, cinnamon, cloves, and baking soda. Mix creamed mixture and flour mixture alternately with coffee. Bake in greased 9x13″ pan at 350° for 45 to 60 minutes.

Cheryl Ladd

Yorkshire Pudding

by June Lockhart

Yorkshire pudding is as English as the "pound". It is a popover-type bread with the wonderful flavor of the Prime Rib.

Serves: 6 to 8
Oven: 425°

Ingredients:

1 cup flour
1 teaspoon salt
1 cup milk

2 eggs
1 teaspoon melted butter
¼ cup meat drippings

Directions:

Combine flour, salt and milk. Beat. Add eggs, one at a time, beating well after each addition. Chill batter. Pour ¼ cup pan drippings into a greased 8x8″ pan.

Set pan in oven to heat.

Pour batter into sizzling pan and bake at 400° for 30 minutes, or until firm and slightly brown. Cut pudding into squares and place on platter with meat.

June Lockhart

Almond Meringue Cookies

by Mary Tyler Moore

"One cookie equals 32 calories." That's good news for calorie counters with a sweet tooth.

Yields: 2 to 2½ dozen
Oven: 275°

Ingredients:

4 egg whites
8 tablespoons powdered
   skim milk
1 teaspoon vanilla extract

1 teaspoon almond extract
1 teaspoon liquid artificial
   sweetener
cinnamon

Directions:

Beat egg whites until stiff. Add skim milk powder. Mix well. Add extracts and sugar substitute.

Drop cookies by spoonfuls onto cookie sheet. Bake at 275° for 45 minutes. Remove from cookie sheet and dust with cinnamon.

Mary Tyler Moore

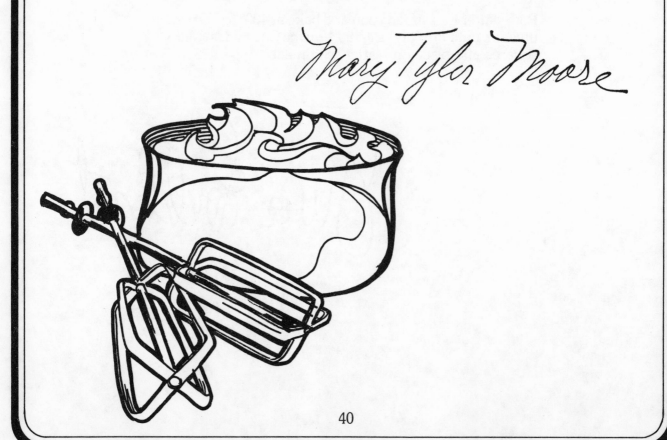

40

Lemon Layer Bars

by Trusse Norris

"I do eat more than I should whenever my wife fixes it."

Yield: 36 bars
Oven: 350°

Ingredients:

1 pkg. (18½ oz.) lemon or
   yellow cake mix
½ cup butter or margarine,
   melted
2 eggs

1 pkg. (3 oz.) lemon pudding
   and pie filling mix
1 can (14 oz.) sweetened
   condensed milk
1⅓ cups flaked coconut
¼ cup nutmeats, chopped

Directions:

In large mixing bowl, combine dry cake mix, butter and eggs. By hand, stir until dough holds together. Press in ungreased 9x13" pan or 15x10x1" jelly roll pan.

Combine pudding mix and sweetened condensed milk. Mix well. Spread over dough in pan. Sprinkle with coconut and nutmeats. Bake at 350° for 20 to 30 minutes until golden brown. Cool and cut into bars.

Cream Cheese Cookies

by Carl Reiner

Everybody loves a butter cookie! Cream cheese and walnuts make this even more "melt-in-your-mouth!"

Yield: about 48 cookies
Oven: 350°

Ingredients:

4 oz. cream cheese
½ cup butter or margarine
9 tablespoons sugar

9 walnut halves, finely
    chopped
1 cup flour

Directions:

Cream the cheese and butter in a bowl. Add sugar gradually, cream after each tablespoon. Add chopped walnuts. Fold in flour and mix until smooth.

Drop mixture by teaspoonfuls onto a cookie sheet. Flatten each cookie as thin as possible, using fingers that have been dipped in cold water.

Bake at 350° for 10 minutes or until cookies are light tan around the edges.

Carl Reiner

Whole Wheat Waffles

by Joni Robbins

These waffles feature very nutritious ingredients. They are delicious served with honey and butter.

Serves: 4 to 6

Ingredients:

2 eggs
2 cups whole wheat flour
1½ cups water

1 cup raisins and/or
   sunflower seeds,
   sesame seeds or granola
¼ teaspoon salt

Directions:

Separate eggs. Beat egg whites until stiff. In a large mixing bowl, mix the egg yolks, flour, water and salt. Add raisins or sesame seeds or sunflower seeds or granola.

Fold in beaten egg whites. Cook in a greased hot waffle iron, until done.

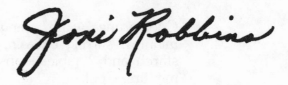

Prune Pie

by Dick Ryan

Serves: 6 to 8
Oven: 375°

Pie baking is easy these days with many baked pie shells available in the grocery stores. Enjoy this orange-prune meringue pie.

Ingredients:

1 9″ baked pie shell	2 tablespoons butter or margarine
2 cups prunes, pitted and cut lengthwise	2 tablespoons cornstarch
1 cup water	2 tablespoons cold water
1 medium orange, peeled and diced	2 egg whites
½ cup sugar	¼ teaspoon cream of tartar
½ teaspoon salt	3½ tablespoons sugar
	few drops of lemon extract

Directions:

Cook prunes, water, orange, sugar and salt. Cook for 30 minutes, stirring occasionally. Add butter. Mix cornstarch and 2 tablespoons cold water. Add to prune mixture. Cool.

Beat egg whites until foamy. Add cream of tartar. Beat. Add sugar very slowly while beating. Add lemon extract and beat until it stands in peaks.

Add filling mixture to baked pie shell. Cover with meringue. Bake in a 375° oven until meringue is browned, approximately 10 minutes.

Dick Ryan.

Date Nut Bread

by Deena Deardurff Schmidt

This quick bread is a favorite for any meal anytime of the year!

Yield: 2 loaves or
4 1lb. loaves
Oven: 325°

Ingredients:

1 cup pitted dates, chopped
2 teaspoons baking soda
2 cups boiling water
2 cups sugar
2 tablespoons butter or
   margarine

2 eggs
1 cup walnuts, chopped
4 cups flour
2 teaspoons salt
2 teaspoons vanilla

Directions:

Combine dates, baking soda and boiling water. Let cool.

Cream together, sugar, butter, eggs, walnuts, flour, salt and vanilla. Add date mixture.

Divide into 2 greased loaf pans or 4 greased 1-lb. cans. Fill about ½ full. Bake at 325° for 1 hour.

Deena Deardurff Schmidt

45

Sugar Cookies

by Eunice Kennedy Shriver

Have you ever met a kid who didn't adore sugar cookies?
No cookbook would be complete without a special cookie
recipe.

Yield: About 3 Doz.
Oven: 375°

Ingredients:

½ cup butter
¾ cup sugar
1 egg
½ teaspoon vanilla
1 tablespoon cream (heavy)

1¼ cups flour
¼ teaspoon salt
¼ teaspoon baking powder
additional butter and sugar

Directions:

Cream butter until light and fluffy. Beat in sugar. Add egg
and vanilla and beat thoroughly. Add cream. Sift together salt, flour and baking powder and add to mixture.
Mix well.

Drop by teaspoonfuls on cookie sheet 1" apart. Bake 8
minutes at 375°.

After baking, brush with butter and sprinkle with sugar.

Eunice Kennedy Shriver

A NEW KIND OF JOY

Coconut Buttermilk Cake

by Bart Starr

Crown this three layer coconut cake with a boiled icing and additional coconut. Whipped cream also would be good.

Serves: 12 to 16
Oven: 375°

Ingredients:

½ cup butter or margarine
½ cup shortening
2 cups sugar
5 eggs, separated
1 teaspoon vanilla
2 cups sifted all-purpose flour

1 teaspoon soda
½ teaspoon salt
1 cup buttermilk
1 can (3½ oz.) flaked coconut
1 cup chopped pecans

Directions:

Cream margarine and shortening until light and fluffy. Add 1½ cups sugar gradually; beat again until light and fluffy. Add egg yolks and vanilla; beat thoroughly.

Add flour sifted with soda and salt in thirds alternately with buttermilk, beating until smooth after each addition.

Turn batter into a 3-quart mixing bowl.

Beat egg whites until stiff but not dry; beat remaining ½ cup sugar in gradually. Fold egg whites into batter gently but thoroughly. Fold in coconut and pecans.

Spread batter in 3 greased, wax paper-lined, and again greased 9" cake pans or 9x13" well-greased pan.

Bake at 375° for about 25 minutes, or until brown.

Fill and frost as you wish.

Bart Starr

Chocolate Cherry Cake

by Hank Stram

Do you like chocolate covered cherries? It's a sure bet you'll love this chocolate cherry cake.

Serves: 8 to 10
Oven: 350°

Ingredients:

½ cup butter or margarine
1 egg
1 cup sugar
1 square unsweetened chocolate
1½ cups flour
1 teaspoon soda
½ teaspoon salt

1 cup buttermilk
4 oz. maraschino cherries, cut up (and juice)
½ cup nuts, chopped

Directions:

Cream together butter, egg and sugar. Melt chocolate and add to the butter mixture.

Sift together flour, soda and salt. Add to butter and chocolate mixture. Add buttermilk and beat well. Add cherries, juice and nuts. Mix well.

Pour into a greased and floured 8x8″ or 9x9″ pan. Bake at 350° for 10 minutes. Lower heat to 325° and bake for about 30 minutes. Sprinkle with powdered sugar or frost if you like.

Heavenly Pancakes

by John West

"If you want to be adventurous, try warming the maple syrup and add 1 or 2 oz. of brandy. This is known as 'mystery' syrup."

Serves: 6 to 8

Ingredients:

1 cup sour cream	1 tablespoon sugar
1 cup cottage cheese	½ teaspoon salt
4 eggs, separated	¾ cup flour
1 teaspoon vanilla	

Directions:

Mix all ingredients with exception of egg whites. Mix thoroughly. Beat egg whites until stiff and fold into mixture. Spoon batter onto hot griddle, being careful not to make the pancakes too large. Serve with pure maple syrup.

John West

SPECIAL OLYMPICS OFFICIAL

Hand-Me-Down Fruitcake

by Marilyn E. White

Chocolate chips are a surprise ingredient in a traditional fruitcake recipe that's a family favorite.

Serves: 15 to 20
Oven: 300°

Ingredients:

½ cup brandy
1 teaspoon orange extract
1 pkg. (2¾ oz.) blanched slivered almonds
1½ cups candied fruit
1 pkg. (6 oz.) chocolate chips
2 cups sifted flour

2 teaspoons baking powder
¼ teaspoon baking soda
½ teaspoon salt
1 cup butter or margarine
1 cup sugar
¾ cup dark brown sugar
5 eggs

Directions:

Combine extract, brandy, candied fruit, almonds and chocolate chips. Soak at least ½ hour. Sift together flour, baking powder, baking soda and salt. Set aside.

Cream butter, adding granulated and brown sugar. Beat until very light. Beat eggs into mixture one at a time.

Gradually add flour mixture to butter mixture and beat well. Carefully fold in brandy mixture.

Pour into a well greased and floured 10x5″ loaf pan. Bake at 300° for 80 to 90 minutes or until firm on top. Cool in pan for 15 minutes, turn out on wire rack.

When completely cooled, wrap in plastic or foil and store in refrigerator 24 to 48 hours before serving. If desired cake can be basted again with brandy.

Marilyn E. White

THREE

Desserts

Flan (Custard) by Eddie Albert

Flan is a favorite dessert from Europe and you'll love its versatility with fruit in season.

Serves: 6 to 8
Oven: 350°

Caramel:

6 tablespoons sugar
4 tablespoons water

Filling:

5 eggs
1 cup water
1 teaspoon vanilla
1 can (14 oz.) sweetened
    condensed milk
various fruits, if desired
fresh mint, if desired

Directions:

To make caramel; cook sugar and water over moderately high heat (about 3 to 4 minutes) until it reaches a light, nut brown color. Stir occasionally.

Line a warm, lightly greased 9″ or 10″ pie plate with caramel mixture working quickly using a swirling motion to coat dish evenly. Set aside.

In bowl, beat 5 eggs. Add 1 cup of water and vanilla. Beat well with wisk. Add condensed milk and beat again. Pour mixture into caramel coated dish.

Place dish in a larger pan half filled with hot water. Bake at 350° for 1 hour and 15 minutes. Check for doneness with a toothpick. If toothpick comes out clean, the Flan is ready. Cool.

When cooled, turn Flan over onto a serving plate. If desired, decorate with various fruits and mint.

Eddie Albert

Fruit Crisp

by Shirley Boone

A fruit crisp so versatile you can use your favorite fruit.

Serves: 8 to 10
Oven: 375°

CRUST

Ingredients:

⅔ cup butter or margarine,
   melted
1½ cups oatmeal
½ cup unbleached flour
¾ cup honey

Directions:

Melt butter and mix the crust ingredients. Set aside.

FILLING

Ingredients:

2½ cups fruit, pared and
   sliced for apples, add
   1 teaspoon cinnamon,
   for peaches or
   apricots, add ½
   teaspoon nutmeg,
   allspice or cloves, for
   prunes or plums add ½
   teaspoon cloves.
¼ cup unbleached flour
¼ cup butter or margarine

Mix the filling.

Layer one half of the crust in a 9x9 or 8x8" pan. Press down firmly. Combine fruit and flour; spread over crust. Dot fruit layer with remaining crust mixture and butter. Bake at 375° for 30 to 40 minutes.

Shirley Boone

Blueberry Souffle

by Florence Henderson

Blueberry lovers wish they had their own blueberry patch. This dessert will make you join the group.

Serves: 6
Oven: 350°

Ingredients:

1 cup blueberries	4 egg yolks
1 cup heavy cream	½ cup sugar
2 tablespoons butter or margarine	6 egg whites
3 tablespoons flour	crushed blueberries and ice cream or Kirsch or cognac-flavored whipped cream, if desired
1 teaspoon grated lemon rind	
2 teaspoons lemon juice	

Directions:

Crush berries and add enough heavy cream to make 1¾ cups.

Melt butter; add flour. Cook a moment or two and then add berry-cream. Cook until thick, stirring constantly. Remove from heat and add lemon rind and juice.

Beat egg yolks with ¼ cup of the sugar and add them to the blueberry mixture.

Beat egg whites and gradually add the remaining ¼ cup of sugar and beat until stiff. Blend in blueberry mixture and turn into a buttered and sugared 1 quart souffle dish.

Bake at 350° for 25 to 30 minutes. Serve at once. Serve with additional crushed berries which you have mixed with the ice cream or sweetened and flavored (Kirsch or cognac) whipped cream. (Whipped cream should be very cold.)

Florence Henderson

Natural Delight

by Peter Lupus

What is more delicious than fresh fruit in season! This dessert or snack combines fruit, natural foods and frozen yogurt.

Serves: 6

Ingredients:

1 medium cantaloupe
¼ whole watermelon
3 medium peaches
3 medium apples
½ whole pineapple

¼ cup almonds, chopped
½ cup raisins
½ cup sunflower seeds, unsalted
1 quart low calorie frozen yogurt

Directions:

Chop fruits into bite size pieces and mix together in a large bowl. In a separate bowl, mix together almonds, raisins and sunflower seeds (reserving some).

Toss mixture together and place in separate serving dishes. Sprinkle remaining nut mixture on top. Add one scoop of yogurt to each serving and place in freezer 3 to 5 minutes before serving.

Peter Lupus

I PARTICIPATE IN SPECIAL OLYMPICS

Dessert Pizza Flambe

by Karen Lustgarten

If you like to serve dessert with a flare, this is one you should try. Fruit, nuts and chocolate are flambed with orange liqueur.

Serves: 6
Oven: 350°

Ingredients:

1 8" to 9" baked pie shell
1 carton (8 oz.) plain or fruit
    yogurt *or* 1 carton
    (8 oz.) sour cream *or*
    a mixture of both
3 to 4 cups mixed fresh
    fruits (your favorite
    combination)

½ cup chopped nuts
½ cup chocolate bits
1 to 2 tablespoons honey
¼ to ½ cup Grand Marnier
    (or any 80 proof orange
    liqueur)

Directions:

Stir yogurt (or sour cream) in carton to loosen. Spread into baked pie shell. Pile fruit on top and spread evenly. Sprinkle nuts and chocolate bits over top. ("Amount really depends on your sweet tooth or calorie allowance, just don't overdo it!") Place pie in 350° oven for approx. 3 minutes to warm.

While pie is in oven, heat liqueur in a small pan on low heat until it starts to bubble. Remove pie from oven and place on table. Ignite liqueur with a match and while it flames, pour evenly over pie.

"Voila!"

Karen Lustgarten

Ice Cream Torte with Fudge Sauce

by Meredith MacRae

These special tips make this a special dessert for all seasons. "The torte will keep for a month in the freezer if well wrapped. Cut off the necessary number of slices whenever you need a quick dessert. The sauce will keep in the refrigerator for weeks."

Serves: 8

Ingredients:

1 qt. dark chocolate ice cream

1 qt. mocha ice cream, or any other flavor of your choice

1 cup semisweet chocolate bits

1 cup heavy cream

½ teaspoon dry instant coffee

1 tablespoon dark rum, cognac or brandy

35 to 40 chocolate wafers, crushed with a rolling pin or 1½ cups crushed macaroons

½ lb. English toffee candy (Almond Roca), chopped coarsely

Directions:

Set out both quarts of ice cream to let them soften slightly while you make the sauce.

Melt the chocolate pieces with the cream and the coffee in a small, heavy saucepan over low heat, stirring until smooth. Remove from heat and stir in rum, cognac or brandy. Set aside until needed. (This sauce may be served warm or at room temperature.)

CONTINUED —

Ice Cream Torte with Fudge Sauce

by Meredith MacRae

Oil the spring-form pan and spread half the crushed cookies on the bottom. When the ice cream is soft enough to be workable, spread the chocolate ice cream carefully on top of the crushed cookie crumbs. Drizzle some of the chocolate sauce over the ice cream. Spread the rest of the cookie crumbs over this. Then spread the mocha (or other flavor) ice cream over all. Drizzle more chocolate sauce on top (reserve some sauce to serve with the torte), then distribute the crushed English toffee evenly over the surface.

Place the torte in the freezer for at least 3 hours until hardened. Remove the spring-form sides of the pan about 5 minutes before serving and let the torte rest at room temperature so it will be easier to slice. Gently reheat the sauce if desired.

Meredith MacRae

SPECIAL OLYMPICS VOLUNTEER

Peach Cobbler

by Alan Page

Fresh sliced peaches nestled on a rich cobbler bake to perfection — Um! — what could be better!

Serves: 6
Oven: 350°

Ingredients:

¾ cup flour
⅛ teaspoon salt
2 teaspoons baking powder
1 cup sugar
¾ cup milk or half and half

½ cup butter, melted
2 cups peeled fresh
    peaches, sliced
1 cup sugar

Directions:

In bowl, sift flour, salt and baking powder. Add 1 cup sugar and milk to make batter. Stir. Melt butter in 8x8x2" baking pan. Pour batter over melted butter. Do *not* stir.

Mix peaches and 1 cup sugar; carefully spoon over batter. Bake 1 hour at 350°. Serve hot or cold, with or without cream.

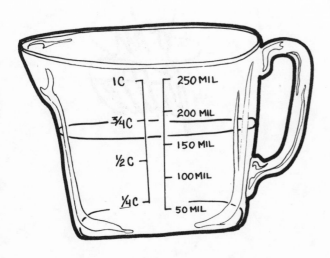

Favorite Fudge
by John Ritter

Fudge is an all-American favorite! This recipe is a family affair. It belongs to Nancy Morgan Ritter's father and they say, "Lick spoons and pan."

Ingredients:

2 cups sugar
3 or 4 heaping tablespoons cocoa
1 cup milk

1½ tablespoons butter or margarine
1 teaspoon vanilla

Directions:

Combine sugar and cocoa; mix thoroughly. Add milk, stirring until mixture is smooth. Heat until mixture comes to boiling. Continue slow boil, stirring only occasionally to remove mixture from sides of pan. Cook to soft-ball stage (238°).

Remove from heat. Allow to cool for 5 minutes. Then stir in butter and vanilla.

Beat hard until fudge becomes very thick and starts to loose its gloss. Pour on buttered plate.

Floating Islands by Sargent Shriver

The French enjoy this dessert and call it "Oeuff a la Neige." Puffs of meringue "float" on a custard sauce. Ambassador Shriver wishes you "Bon Appetit."

Serves: 6

MERINGUE TOPPING

Ingredients:

> 5 egg whites (reserve the yolks)
> ⅝ cup sugar

Directions:

> Beat egg whites until foamy. Gradually add sugar, continuing to beat until whites are stiff.
>
> Use an ice cream scooper to make scoops of the egg whites. Drop these scoops into a large skillet with simmering — not boiling — water. Poach on each side, about a minute or until set. Remove meringues to a towel and drain. Serve with the following sauce.

SAUCE

Ingredients:

> 8 egg yolks
> 1 qt. light cream
> 2 tablespoons sugar
> 4 tablespoons vanilla

Directions:

> Scald the cream, sugar, and vanilla in top of a double boiler. Beat the eggs into this, stirring constantly until thick.
>
> To cool the sauce, place meringues on top and chill.

Sargent Shriver

Fruit Sherbet

by Sally Struthers

Serves: 4 to 8

A sherbet as easy as turning on your blender and pouring in a freezer dish! Wow, what a fresh fruit taste.

Ingredients:

juice of 1 lemon	1 cup frozen strawberries
juice of 1 orange	¾ cup sugar
1 ripe banana, mashed	1 cup half and half

Directions:

Mix all ingredients thoroughly. Can use a blender. Pour into an 8x8" square pan. Freeze. Stir once or twice during first hour.

Sally Struthers

I'M A LOVER OF SPECIAL KIDS

Chocolate Souffle

by Marlo Thomas

What could be a more perfect climax to dinner than a
light and airy chocolate souffle!

Serves: 6
Oven: 375°

Ingredients:

2 tablespoons butter
2 tablespoons flour
¾ cup milk
pinch of salt
2 squares unsweetened
    chocolate

⅓ cup sugar
2 tablespoons cold coffee
½ teaspoon vanilla extract
3 egg yolks, lightly beaten
4 egg whites, stiffly beaten
whipped cream

Directions:

In a saucepan melt the butter, add the flour and stir with a
wire whisk until blended. Meanwhile, in a separate pan,
bring the milk to a boil and add all at once to the butter-
flour mixture, stirring vigorously with the whisk. Add the
salt.

Melt the chocolate with the sugar and coffee over hot
water. Stir the melted chocolate mixture into the sauce
and add the vanilla. Beat in the egg yolks, one at a time,
and cool.

Fold in the stiffly beaten egg whites and turn the mixture
into a buttered 2-quart casserole sprinkled with sugar.
Bake at 375° for 35 to 45 minutes, or until puffed and
brown. Serve immediately with whipped cream.

Marlo Thomas

FOUR

Eggs and Cheese Dishes

Special Scrambled Eggs

by Richard Anderson

The combination of salami and Swiss cheese make these scrambled eggs special.

Serves: 2 to 3

Ingredients:

¼ cup butter or margarine
2 medium onions, coarsely chopped
6 extra large eggs
½ cup milk
½ cup salami, diced

½ cup Swiss cheese, grated
2 tablespoons butter or margarine
tomato slices, for garnish
watercress, for garnish

Directions:

Melt ¼ cup butter in medium skillet. Add onions and cook over medium heat until brown. Set aside.

Beat eggs with milk. Add salami, Swiss cheese and onions. Melt 2 tablespoons of butter in skillet. Add egg mixture and scramble 'til set. Serve immediately with tomato slices and watercress.

Great American Omelette

by Terry Bradshaw and JoJo Starbuck Bradshaw

"This is great for a Sunday brunch with a salad and hot rolls. I hope others will enjoy this omelette as much as Terry and I have."

Serves: 4 to 6

Ingredients:

½ lb. hot sausage
1 to 2 tablespoons butter
1 small to medium
   zucchini, chopped
1 stalk broccoli, chopped
1 cup mushrooms, sliced
   lengthwise
8 eggs
½ cup white wine or water

½ cup cottage cheese
½ lb. Muenster cheese,
   chopped
⅛ teaspoon Tabasco
½ teaspoon seasoned salt
¼ teaspoon pepper, freshly
   ground
1 teaspoon sweet basil
¼ teaspoon dill

Directions:

Fry sausage and drain. In a large skillet, melt butter. Saute zucchini, broccoli and mushrooms. Add drained sausage.

In a bowl mix eggs, wine or water, cheese and seasonings. Pour over hot vegetables and sausage.

Cook a few minutes, stirring slightly. Turn heat down and steam with lid on a few minutes until cooked through and slightly soft.

Note: Instead of hot sausage you may add cooked bacon, shrimp, lobster, chopped green or red peppers.

JoJo ✳︎ ♯ Bradshaw

Terry Bradshaw

"Plains Special" Cheese Ring

by Rosalynn Carter

This unusual cheese ring can star at many eating occasions — dessert, afternoon tea or coffee or even with a glass of wine.

Yield: 1 ring

Ingredients:

1 lb. shredded sharp cheese
1 cup finely chopped nuts
1 cup mayonnaise
1 small onion, finely grated

black pepper
dash cayenne
strawberry preserves, if desired
plain crackers

Directions:

Combine all ingredients except preserves, season to taste with pepper. Mix well and place in a 5 or 6 cup lightly greased ring mold. Refrigerate until firm for several hours or overnight.

To serve, unmold, and if desired, fill center with strawberry preserves, or serve plain with crackers.

Rosalynn Carter

Mozzarella Marinara

by Shari Lewis

A cheese lover's dream — crusty slices of sauteed mozzarella cheese nestled in tomato sauce and topped with an anchovy strip.

Serves: 4 to 6

Ingredients:

16 oz. mozzarella cheese,
   sliced into ½″ slices
½ cup flour
2 eggs, slightly beaten
1 cup herbed and seasoned
   bread crumbs

olive oil
1 can (10½ oz.) pizza sauce
1 can (2 oz.) flat anchovies

Directions:

Dip each slice of cheese into egg, then flour, then back into egg (and make sure you wet all of the floured surface) and then into the bread crumbs. Pack the bread crumbs against the surface of the cheese so it forms a good crust.

Place the slices on a plate ("I use a paper plate") and either put in the freezer for 20 minutes or the refrigerator for an hour.

Pour ¼″ of olive oil in a frying pan. When oil is very hot, place the cold cheese slices into the oil, and allow to brown crisply on each side. Heat the pizza sauce in a small saucepan. When cheese slices are crisp and just beginning to ooze through the crust, carefully lift them out of the pan. Place on paper toweling to drain.

On each serving dish, place a large tablespoon of the warmed sauce, a slice of fried cheese, another tablespoon of sauce and a strip of anchovy. Serve.

"I'm an anchovy freak, so I top it with two anchovies."

Shari Lewis

69

Cheesy-Good Omelet

by Merlin Olsen

A three egg omelet with a special combination of flavors and a cheese filling. A special meal any time of the day.

Serves: 1

Ingredients:

1 tablespoon butter or margarine, melted
1 tablespoon onion, chopped
2 tablespoons chopped mushrooms
2 tablespoons chopped green pepper
1½ tablespoons butter or margarine, melted

3 eggs
2 tablespoons milk or cream
½ teaspoon salt
1 tablespoon chopped parsley
dash of Tabasco
⅓ cup shredded sharp Cheddar cheese

Directions:

Saute onion, mushrooms and green pepper in 1 tablespoon butter. Set aside.

Beat 3 eggs. Add milk or cream, salt, and Tabasco. Heat omelet pan and add 1½ tablespoons butter. When butter is bubbling, pour in egg mixture. Gently stir. Add onion, mushrooms, green pepper, and parsley. Continue to stir.

When the omelet is just set (do not cook too long) sprinkle the cheese down the center and fold. Turn out onto warm plate. Serve at once.

Merlin Olsen

Welsh Rabbit

by Joan Rivers

A cheese lover's special brunch or luncheon dish.   **Serves: 4 to 5**

Ingredients:

4 tablespoons butter or
    margarine
¼ cup flour
½ teaspoon salt
¼ teaspoon pepper
¼ teaspoon dry mustard

1 can (12 oz.) vegetable
    juice
1 cup processed American
    cheese, grated
crackers, English muffins
    or toast

Directions:

Melt butter in chafing dish pan. Stir in flour gradually. Add salt, pepper and mustard. Mix. Add vegetable juice slowly, stirring constantly. Bring to boil, stirring continually.

Cook 2 minutes. Add cheese and stir until melted. Serve at once on crackers, toast or split and toasted English muffin.

Quiche Lorraine by Isabel Sanford

A basic French cheese pie which gives the baker a choice
of fillings.

Serves: 6 to 8
Oven: 400°

Ingredients:

4 eggs
2 cups half and half
½ teaspoon salt
¼ teaspoon pepper
dash nutmeg
dash garlic powder
1 cup shredded Swiss
    cheese
2 unbaked pie shells

Filling Choices:

canned shrimp, drained
crabmeat, drained
bacon, fried and drained
boiled ham, chopped
spinach, chopped

Directions:

In bowl, mix eggs and half and half together by hand. Add
spices and fold in cheese. Fold in your choice of filling.

Pour in unbaked pie shells. Bake at 400° for 30 minutes.
Test doneness by inserting knife in center of pie; if knife
comes out clean, the pie is done.

Isabel Sanford
Weezy

Open Faced Egg Sandwich(or Late-Nite Delight)

by Bobby Smith

Be a hit the next time your "on" to serve the late night snack. This is a delicious hot sandwich, especially after National Hockey League action.

Serves: 6
Oven: 350°

Ingredients:

6 hard cooked eggs
¼ cup mayonnaise
2 tablespoons celery, chopped
1 tablespoon onion, chopped
salt and pepper to taste

6 slices bread (I prefer brown bread)
6 slices ham or 12 slices fried bacon
1 cup shredded Cheddar cheese

Directions:

Chop eggs and add mayonnaise, celery, onion, salt and pepper. In oven, toast bread on *one* side. Place egg mixture on *untoasted* side of bread. Top with ham slices or two slices of fried bacon. Generously sprinkle with Cheddar cheese. Place in 350° oven until cheese is bubbly.

Bobby Smith

Egg in the Nest

by James Stacy

A "neat" way to have an egg and toast for breakfast.

Serves: 1

Ingredients:

1 slice of favorite bread   **salt and pepper to taste**
1 egg

Directions:

Lightly grease frying pan and heat. Poke a "silver dollar" size hole in middle of bread. Lay bread in pan and fry for 20 seconds on one side. Crack egg into hole of bread. Cook egg until desired doneness. Flip. Cook for an additional 20 to 30 seconds.

James Stacy

FIVE

Fish and Seafood

Barbecued Trout

by Hal Baylor

Hal Baylor says about his favorite fish recipe: "Remove bones, and eat your heart out!"

Serves: 4

Ingredients:

4 trout (1 to 1½ lbs.)
1½ cups oil
½ cup soy sauce

3 cloves garlic, minced
dehydrated parsley flakes

Directions:

Clean trout and remove heads. Combine oil, soy sauce and garlic. Add trout and marinate for 8 hours. Turn trout every couple of hours.

Place in a flat hamburger rack. Sprinkle with dehydrated parsley flakes. Salt and pepper to your own taste.

Place on a regular barbecue grill over low coals and cook approximately 2 minutes on each side. Serve with lemon slices or homemade tartar sauce.

Hal Baylor

Broiled Deviled Clams

by Carol Burnett

A delicious topping makes these deviled clams very special.

Serves: 6

Ingredients:

24 small hard-shelled
   clams
¾ cup butter or margarine,
   softened
¼ cup shallots, minced
2 to 3 tablespoons Dijon-
   style mustard

2 tablespoons lemon juice
salt and pepper to taste
dry bread crumbs
rock salt

Directions:

Clean and shuck clams, discarding the top shell, and release them from the bottom shells. In a bowl combine the butter, shallots, mustard, lemon juice, salt and pepper.

Divide the butter mixture among the clams, spreading it evenly over each clam, so clam is completely covered. Cover the clams with plastic wrap and chill 30 minutes.

Sprinkle 2 teaspoons bread crumbs over each clam and arrange the clams on a bed of rock salt in a shallow baking pan. Broil clams 2″ from flame for 3 to 4 minutes until the crumbs are golden.

Carol Burnett

Dilled Bay Scallops

by David Cassidy

If you love fish, treat yourself to a marvelous scallop bake. The dill weed adds flavor excitement.

Serves: 2 to 3

Ingredients:

1 lb. bay scallops
2 tablespoons butter or margarine
1 can condensed cream of shrimp or cream of mushroom soup, undiluted

¼ cup half & half
2 tablespoons chablis or sauterne wine
1 teaspoon dill weed
grated Parmesan cheese

Directions:

Brown scallops in butter in skillet. Add soup, half & half, wine and dill. Cook for a few minutes. Remove from skillet and place in a shallow baking dish or individual baking shells. Then top with grated cheese. Broil briefly until top is light brown, and serve.

Rocky Mountain Campfire Trout

by Billy Kidd

"There are three ways to cook this trout. The best way is on the shore of a high mountain lake or stream, however, it can also be excellent cooked on your outdoor barbecue. The third method is cooking the fish in an oven for 10 minutes at 375°, also producing great results."

Serves: 1

Ingredients:

1 medium sized Rocky
    Mountain trout,
    approx. 1 lb.
1 teaspoon butter
1 lemon

salt and pepper to taste
Dijon-style mustard
bay leaf, if desired
fresh parsley, chopped

Directions:

Put a teaspoon of butter and a slice of lemon inside each fish. Spread with butter and squeeze lemon juice on both sides. Spread both sides with mustard and place a bay leaf inside the trout. Sprinkle with salt and pepper inside and out.

Wrap fish with aluminum foil and place on grill over hot coals, making sure that foil is not torn or wrapped too tightly. In this way the foil serves as an oven. Cook for about 15 to 20 minutes.

The readiness is indicated by the flakey texture of the flesh. Remove foil, sprinkle fish with chopped parsley and serve with melted butter and lemon wedges.

Scampi

by Walter Lantz

Who can resist a shrimp dinner; especially one prepared with this special recipe?

Serves: 4

Ingredients:

16 medium size shrimp, in the shell
¼ cup butter
4 tablespoons olive oil

3 teaspoons garlic powder
½ teaspoon salt
¼ teaspoon white pepper

Directions:

Remove legs from shrimp. Split shrimp in underside leaving on shell and tail. Melt butter in frying pan. Add oil, garlic powder, salt and pepper. Add shrimp. Cover and saute for 5 minutes or until shrimp are pink.

Walter Lantz

OIL

Papaya-Crab Supreme

by Ross Martin

Serves: 4

A simple salad with wonderful foods of the South Pacific.
Don't wait until you go to Hawaii to enjoy it!

Ingredients:

2 fresh papayas, chilled
²/₃ cup celery, thinly sliced
1 can (6½ oz.) crabmeat, flaked
juice of ½ lime

½ cup toasted slivered almonds
fresh parsley or mint leaves

Directions:

Mix crabmeat with celery and chill. Cut papayas in halves and remove seeds. Place on individual shells or salad plates. Squeeze lime juice on crab mixture. Add almonds and pile in papaya halves. Garnish with parsley sprigs or mint leaves and serve with lime wedges.

Shrimp with Lobster Sauce
by Jayne Meadows

"To serve this dish without meat, you may use minced bamboo shoots, mushrooms or water chestnuts. This is an Americanized Chinese dish. Actually there is no lobster in this dish at all, we just use the same kind of sauce which is used in lobster with meat sauce."

Serves: 4 to 6

Ingredients:

1 lb. raw shrimp
2 teaspoons dry sherry
2 tablespoons cornstarch
4 tablespoons cooking oil
2 slices ginger root
2 cloves garlic, crushed
1½ tablespoons black beans, minced

½ cup ground pork, about ¼ lb.
½ teaspoon salt
2 tablespoons soy sauce
¼ teaspoon MSG
¼ teaspoon sugar
1 egg, beaten

Directions:

Rinse and shell shrimp. Remove infestinal vein. Mix shrimp with sherry and ½ tablespoon of cornstarch. Mix the remaining 1½ tablespoons cornstarch with ¼ cup cold water.

Put oil in hot skillet over medium-high heat. Add shrimp and stir constantly for 2 minutes. Remove shrimp and leave as much oil in the skillet as you can.

Return skillet to heat. Add ginger root, garlic and black beans. After a few stirrings; put in pork, salt, soy sauce, MSG, sugar and 1 cup of water. Bring to boil. Cover and simmer for 2 minutes.

Mix the well-stirred cornstarch mixture and the shrimp. Add to skillet mixture. Add beaten egg and gently stir. Serve hot.

Jayne Meadows

Escargot

by Pele

Escargot like your favorite restaurant? Yes, you can have it at home with this recipe!

Serves: 4
Oven: 450°

Ingredients:

1 lb. butter or margarine, softened
½ cups shallots, chopped very fine
2 tablespoons minced garlic
½ cup chopped parsley
pinch of salt and pepper

1 can (4 oz.) snails
2 tablespoons butter or margarine
2 tablespoons shallots, chopped
1 tablespoon minced garlic
1 oz. Ricard or Pernod
1 oz. dry white wine

Directions:

The escargots are prepared in three stages: the escargot butter, the escargot themselves, and final preparation.

To 1 lb. softened butter, add ½ cup shallots, 2 tablespoons garlic, parsley and salt and pepper. Mix well and let stand.

Saute the snails in 2 tablespoons butter, 2 tablespoons shallots and 1 tablespoon garlic for about 5 minutes. Just before removing from heat add 1 oz. Ricard or Pernod.

Remove from heat and allow to cool. Into each escargot shell, stuff a little escargot butter, then add snail and finish stuffing the shell with butter until closed.

Cook the stuffed shells in a 450° oven for about 5 minutes or until the butter is sizzling. Remove from oven and sprinkle a little white wine over the snails. Serve.

Scallops in White Wine Sauce

by Brooks Robinson

Are scallops one of your favorite dishes? This recipe is an exceptional version of the French classic.

Serves: 3 to 4

Ingredients:

1½ lbs. bay scallops
¾ cups dry white wine
3 tablespoons butter or
    margarine
3 tablespoons flour
½ cup cream
1 cup mushrooms, finely
    chopped
salt and pepper, to taste

½ cup cracker crumbs,
    crushed
¾ teaspoon salt
⅛ teaspoon pepper
¼ teaspoon basil
¼ teaspoon oregano
½ teaspoon parsley,
    chopped

Directions:

Put scallops and wine in skillet. Bring to a boil and simmer until tender. Remove scallops and cut into small pieces. Set aside. Add chopped mushrooms to wine and simmer for 3 minutes.

Melt butter in saucepan; stir in flour. Gradually stir in wine and mushroom mixture. Cook over low heat until thickened, stirring constantly. Stir in cream. Add scallops. Add salt and pepper to taste.

Put scallop mixture into buttered individual shells. Combine cracker crumbs with salt, pepper, basil, oregano and parsley. Sprinkle crumb topping on top of filled shells and place under broiler until brown.

Brooks Robinson

Hot Crab Souffle

by Roger Staubach

This is a failure-proof souffle and a marvelous luncheon or supper dish that can be prepared ahead.

Serves: 12
Oven: 325°

Ingredients:

8 slices bread
2 cups crab or shrimp
½ cup mayonnaise
1 onion, chopped
1 green pepper, chopped
1 cup chopped celery

3 cups milk
4 eggs
1 can (10½ oz.) mushroom
    soup
grated cheese

Directions:

Dice half of bread and place in greased 2 quart baking dish. Mix crab or shrimp, mayonnaise, onion, green pepper and celery and spread over diced bread. Trim crusts from remaining four slices and place trimmed slices over shrimp or crab mixture.

Mix eggs and milk together and pour over mixture. Place in refrigerator overnight.

Bake in 325° oven for 15 minutes. Take from oven and pour soup over the top. Top with cheese and paprika. Bake 1 hour in 325° oven.

Roger Staubach

SIX

Lunches and
Supper Dishes

Cottage Cheese and Noodle Kugel

by Edward Asner

An unusual "old world" recipe. That suggests trying it to know how delicious it is!

Serves: 8 to 10
Oven: 350°

Ingredients:

1 pkg. (12 oz.) egg noodles
4 eggs
½ cup sugar
½ teaspoon salt
1 carton (16 oz.) small curd
    cottage cheese
1 carton (16 oz.) sour
    cream

¾ cup butter, melted
1 can (8 oz.) crushed
    pineapple, drained
1 teaspoon sugar
1 teaspoon cinnamon

Directions:

In large saucepan, boil the noodles according to package directions in salted water. Rinse with cold water and drain. Mix eggs, ½ cup sugar, salt, cottage cheese, sour cream and butter until smooth. Pour the mixture over the noodles and fold in pineapple.

Pour into buttered 9x13″ baking dish. Mix 1 teaspoon sugar and cinnamon. Sprinkle top of kugel with the cinnamon mixture. Bake at 350° for 1 hour. Serve in squares with sour cream and jam.

I'M A LOVER OF SPECIAL KIDS

Chili

by Jim Backus

Serves: 6 to 8

"My husband, Jimmy, tried cooking exactly once . . . when we were first married. I became ill with the flu and the doctor suggested that he boil me an egg . . . which he did . . . with no water in the pot! Just an egg . . . a pot . . . and a flame! The explosion was violent . . . the aroma no aid to my condition . . . and the expense of scraping, scrubbing and painting the kitchen was so great that he has been barred from that part of the house ever since . . . a penalty that does not upset him."

Henny Backus

Ingredients:

3 tablespoons bacon fat/oil
1 lb. ground round
1 large green pepper, chopped
2 cloves garlic, run through press
1 can (15 oz.) kidney beans
1 medium onion, chopped

2 cans (16 oz.) whole tomatoes
1½ teaspoons salt
3 whole cloves
1 bay leaf
3 tablespoons "good, strong, fresh chili powder"

Directions:

Brown onion, peppers, garlic and meat in bacon fat until brown and crumbly. Add tomatoes, kidney beans, salt, cloves, bay leaf and chili powder. Bring to boil.

Then cook over a very low flame for about 2½ hours, covered. Remove lid and continue cooking until chili reaches the thickness you desire.

"We have added one or all of these at one time or another . . . . .
Leftover stew meat (or cook some especially for this dish)
Toasted saltines
Sour cream (lots of it mixed in and heated.)
If you use all of these, it is a marvelous party dish, which we then serve over rice.

If you don't think it tastes like chili, you're probably right. But I've never been able to come up with a better name for it. Whatever you care to call it . . . we wish we had some right now!!"

Jim Backus AND *Henny Backus*

89

Mom's Special Macaroni

by Rick Barry

Mom's Special can become everyone's favorite tuna salad.

Serves: 6 to 8

Ingredients:

1 pkg. (24 oz.) elbow macaroni
1 can (13 oz.) light tuna, flaked and drained
1 medium cucumber, chopped
1 or 2 medium tomatoes, chopped

1 avocado, chopped
¼ to ½ cup red onion, chopped
salt and pepper to taste
½ to 1 cup mayonnaise
¼ cup wine vinegar

Directions:

Cook macaroni according to package directions. Drain. Pour into a large bowl.

Add tomatoes, cucumbers, avocado, onion and tuna. Mix mayonnaise and vinegar. Add to salad and gently toss. Salt and pepper to taste.

Chill and serve.

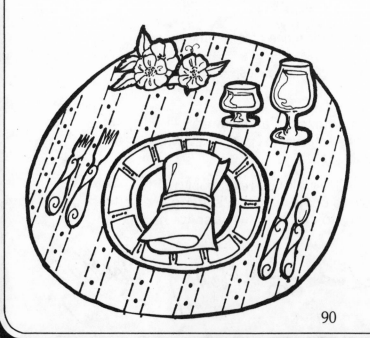

Chili

by Polly Bergen

Polly Bergen gives us a chili that's bound to become a family favorite and the recipe makes enough for guests, too.

Serves: 25

Ingredients:

3 cloves garlic, minced
cooking oil
6 large onions, finely chopped
6 large green peppers, finely chopped
6 lbs. ground round or chuck
5 cans (16 oz. ea.) Italian-style tomatoes
4 to 6 cans (16 oz. ea.) kidney beans, drained
2 cans (6 oz. ea.) tomato paste

salt and pepper to taste
2 teaspoons wine vinegar
5 whole cloves
3 bay leaves
4 tablespoons chili powder (or more to taste)
4 drops Tabasco sauce (or more to taste)
2 teaspoons cumin
1 tablespoon sugar

Directions:

In a large roaster, saute garlic in oil and remove. Saute onions and peppers until golden, remove and drain. Add meat to oil, separate with a fork and cook until all meat is grey in color. Drain off accumulated oil.

Add onions and green peppers to the meat, mix well and then add all of the remaining ingredients. Cover and simmer over low heat for 1 hour. Simmer uncovered for another hour. Remove cloves and bay leaves before serving.

Polly Bergen

Vegetarian Tacos

by Debby Boone

If you're into the "Vegetarian Thing," why not enjoy tacos with a delicious combination of vegetables and cheese.

Serves: 4

Ingredients:

½ cup millet
Tamari or soy sauce
1 avocado, mashed
1 small onion, diced
1 large tomato, chopped

1 to 1¼ cups lettuce, shredded
1 to 1¼ cups shredded Cheddar cheese

Directions:

Add millet to 1¾ cup of water. Stir. Boil slowly for about 20-30 minutes, or until soft. Add a little tamari or soy sauce. Add diced onions to mashed avocado.

Heat the tortillas according to package directions. Assemble the taco beginning with millet and ending with cheese. Fold in half.

Chili

by Pat Boone

Everybody loves chili. This recipe is made different by combining cooked spaghetti with the kidney beans.

Serves: 8

Ingredients:

2 medium onions, chopped
cooking oil
1 lb. ground beef
1 teaspoon salt
1 to 2 tablespoons chili
　　powder

salt to taste
1 can (16 oz.) tomatoes
1 can (16 oz.) tomato sauce
1 can (16 oz.) red kidney
　　beans
4 oz. spaghetti

Directions:

Cook onions in cooking oil until tender. Add ground beef and cook until brown. Drain off fat. Add tomatoes, tomato sauce, kidney beans, chili powder and salt. While chili is simmering, cook spaghetti. Add drained, cooked spaghetti to chili. Simmer for 1 hour.

Pat Boone

Ox Tail Soup

by Todd A. Bridges

A really hearty soup, perfect for a cold winter's night.

Serves: 5 to 6

Ingredients:

4 lbs. ox tails
4 cups water
2 cans (10½ oz. ea.) beef
   broth
1 teaspoon salt
1 teaspoon black pepper

2 garlic cloves, chopped
2 medium onions, chopped
3 carrots, chopped
3 celery sticks, chopped
3 medium potatoes,
   chopped

Directions:

In Dutch oven, combine ox tails, water, beef broth, salt and pepper. Add garlic and onions. Bring to boil. Simmer on low heat about 1 hour. Add chopped carrots and boil for 15 minutes. Add potatoes and celery and boil for 15 more minutes. Ready to serve!

Todd A Bridges

Spiced Macaroni

by Foster Brooks

"All you need is some good Italian bread and a salad. Believe it or not, my family loves whipped potatoes with it."

Serves: 6 to 8
Oven: 300°
or simmer

Ingredients:

1 eye of the round roast or lean chuck roast (3 lbs.)
1 can (29 oz.) tomato puree
1 can (8 oz.) tomato sauce
1 tablespoon pickling spices wrapped and tied in cheesecloth, about the size of a silver dollar

1 dash cinnamon, allspice, nutmeg and cloves (all powdered
1 tablespoon sugar
salt and pepper to taste after cooking for one hour (about 1½ teaspoons salt and ½ teaspoon pepper)
1 pkg. mostaccioli

Directions:

Brown meat on all sides in Dutch oven. Add tomato puree and tomato sauce. Add spice bag, spices and sugar. Simmer for one hour; add salt and pepper to taste.

Add one puree can of water. Simmer until the meat is very tender, about 3 hours. Remove meat and cook sauce to desired thickness, or bake covered at 300° for 3 to 4 hours.

Prepare mostaccioli according to package directions. Drain. Pour mostaccioli into sauce. Stir well and lift from sauce with a slotted spoon into plates or a large serving bowl. Slice meat in ½" slices and serve with mostaccioli and additional sauce.

Foster Brooks

Eggplant and Meat Casserole

by Richard Bull

"Tastes even better the day after. You can bake it for 10 minutes the first day. Refrigerate overnight. Then bake for 10 to 15 minutes and serve."

Serves: 6
Oven: 350°

Ingredients:

1 lb. lean ground beef
1 large eggplant
1 can (28 oz.) tomatoes
2 cups bread crumbs
½ cup grated Parmesan cheese
1 tablespoon parsley, chopped

1 teaspoon oregano
2 cloves garlic, minced
pinch of salt and pepper
½ lb. mozzarella cheese, sliced

Directions:

Brown meat in small amount of oil. Drain and set aside. Peel eggplant and slice into ½" cubes.

Mash tomatoes to a pulp. Mix bread crumbs, Parmesan, parsley, oregano, garlic, salt and pepper.

In a lightly greased 2-quart casserole, layer eggplant, bread crumb mixture, tomatoes and ground beef. Top with mozzarella cheese. Bake at 350° for 30 to 40 minutes. Serve hot.

Fettucine

by Red Buttons

This pasta dish is inspired by some of the finest Italian cuisine.

Serves: 6 to 8

Ingredients:

1 pkg. (16 oz.) noodles	garlic salt, to taste
½ cup butter or margarine, melted	1 cup grated Parmesan cheese
1 pint (8 oz.) sweet cream	dash of vermouth

Directions:

Cook noodles according to package directions. Drain.

Melt butter in large saucepan. Add drained noodles, cream and garlic salt. Mix with two forks.

Add Parmesan cheese and dash of vermouth. Mix well.

Red Buttons

Macaroni Divine

by Saundra Chriss

A tuna, cheese casserole that's sure to become a family favorite.

Serves: 6 to 8
Oven: 350°

Ingredients:

2 cups macaroni
1 2-lb. box Velveeta
   cheese, cubed
1 can (13 oz.) tuna, drained

½ cup celery, chopped
1 medium onion, chopped
1 teaspoon pepper
1 teaspoon paprika

Directions:

Prepare macaroni according to package directions. Drain. Add cheese (reserving some for the top). Add celery, onion, tuna, paprika, and pepper. Mix well.

Bake in greased 2½ to 3 quart casserole. Top with remaining cheese. Sprinkle with additional pepper and paprika on top. Bake at 350° for 20 minutes.

Saundra Chriss

98

Super Supper Tuna Casserole
by Elinor Donahue

Serves: 6 to 8
Oven: 350°

"Great served with petit peas cooked in small amount of water, butter, salt, pepper and basil. Also served with cherry tomatoes vinaigrette."

Ingredients:

1 pkg. (8 oz.) wide egg noodles
1½ cups cottage cheese
1½ cups sour cream
½ cup onion, finely chopped
1 clove garlic, minced
2 teaspoons Worcestershire sauce

½ teaspoon salt
¼ teaspoon pepper
dash of Tabasco
2 cans (6½ oz. ea.) tuna, drained and flaked
½ cup sharp Cheddar cheese, shredded

Directions:

Cook noodles as directed on package. Drain. Combine all ingredients except cheese in a bowl. Blend in cooked noodles. Mix. Spoon mixture into a 2 quart greased casserole. Top with cheese. Bake at 350° for 45 minutes or until bubbly.

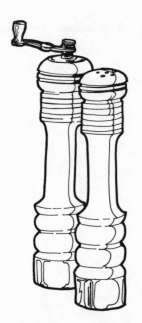

Elinor Donahue

New England Clam Chowder

by Louise Duart

Main dish soups are becoming a family favorite any time of the year.

Serves: 6 to 8

Ingredients:

½ cup onion, chopped
¼ cup butter or margarine
2 cans (10 oz. ea.) whole baby clams with broth
1 can (13 oz.) evaporated milk
2 cups potatoes, cooked and cubed

6 slices bacon, cooked and crumbled
4 cups milk
salt to taste
1 dozen Ritz crackers, crumbled

Directions:

In deep pan, saute onions in butter until golden brown. Add all ingredients except crackers. Heat but do *not* boil.

Cover and remove from heat for 1 hour or more. When ready to serve, reheat and add crumbled Ritz crackers on top of each serving.

Louise Duart

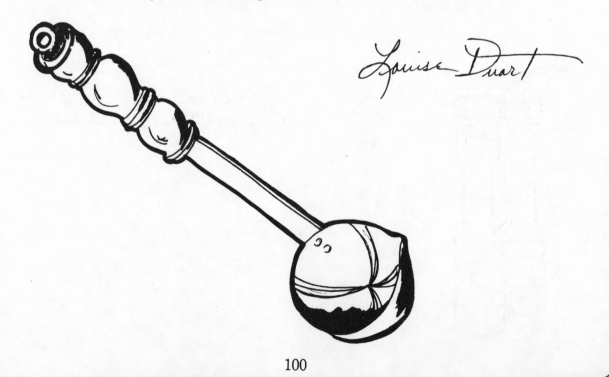

Microwave Pizzaburger Pie
by Geoff Edwards

Dinner in minutes! A pizza-flavored pie that should be a family favorite — especially on really busy days.

Ingredients:

1 lb. lean ground beef
½ cup dry bread crumbs
½ teaspoon oregano
1 teaspoon salt
1 can (8 oz.) tomato sauce
1 pkg. (7 oz.) frozen
    French-fried onion
    rings

1 jar (2½ oz.) sliced
    mushrooms, drained
1 cup shredded mozzarella
    cheese

Directions:

In bowl, combine ground beef, bread crumbs, oregano, salt and ½ cup tomato sauce. Mix gently but thoroughly. Spread evenly in 10″ glass pie plate to form crust.

Cook on HIGH in microwave oven 5 to 6 minutes. Drain off fat. Spread remaining sauce on top of meat, sprinkle with onion rings, mushrooms and cheese. Cook another 5 minutes. Serve immediately.

Creamed Cheese and Vegetable Soup

by Frank Gifford

Homemade soup will make you a star as a hostess any-time. This delicious cheese and vegetable soup is sure to please.

Yield: 2 to 3 quarts

Ingredients:

6 cups chicken broth
1 cup celery, chopped fine
1 cup carrots, chopped fine
1 cup leeks, chopped fine
1 cup broccoli, coarsely
    chopped
½ cup scallions, chopped
    fine

2 tablespoons butter or
    margarine
2 tablespoons flour
1 cup shredded Havarti
    cheese
dash cayenne
sprig parsley
1 cup sweet cream

Directions:

Bring broth to a boil. Add all the vegetables and cook gently about 4 minutes.

Make a "roux" with butter and flour. Drain vegetables, reserving liquid. Add reserved liquid to roux until liquid is a little thick.

Add vegetables and cheese and simmer until cheese is melted. Add cream and cayenne and heat gently. Serve with a sprig of fresh parsley.

Frank Gifford

Chili

By Sandra Giles

Some good cooks like to make their chili with dry beans they cook themselves. This good cook shares her chili which is excellent.

Yield: 4 quarts

Ingredients:

8 oz. dry pinto beans
2 cans (16 oz. ea.) tomatoes
3 tablespoons cooking oil
3 medium green peppers, chopped
2½ cups onion, chopped
2 cloves garlic, minced
½ cup parsley, chopped

½ cup butter or margarine
2½ lbs. ground beef chuck
1 lb. ground pork
3 to 6 tablespoons chili powder (to taste)
2 tablespoons salt
1½ teaspoons pepper
1½ teaspoons cumin seed

Directions:

Wash beans and soak overnight in plenty of water (cover beans with water). Simmer, covered, in the same water (add more if necessary). Simmer for 1 to 2 hours until beans are tender. Add tomatoes and simmer 5 minutes.

Saute green pepper in oil for about 5 minutes. Add onion and saute until tender. Add garlic and parsley.

Melt butter in a large skillet and brown meat. Drain fat. Add cooked meat to green pepper and onion mixture. Add seasonings and cook 10 minutes. Add beans to the meat mixture and simmer covered for 1 hour. Then simmer, uncovered, for 30 minutes. Skim off fat. Freezes well.

Complete Vegetarian

by Arthur Godfrey

"The combination of rice and lentils provides about 35% complete protein. The balance is good vegetable carbohydrate, minerals, vitamins and no fat. It may be served hot as a vegetable or chilled and mixed with any salad as a main course."

Serves: 4

Ingredients:

²/₃ cup brown rice
¹/₃ cup lentils
1²/₃ cups water

1 teaspoon tamari sauce
    or soy sauce
1 teaspoon olive oil

Directions:

Soak rice and lentils in lightly salted water overnight. Add tamari sauce and olive oil. Cover and simmer until all the water is absorbed, about 15 to 20 minutes.

"My favorite dish is to pan-fry thinly sliced fresh vegetables while the rice is cooking — then mix the rice and serve together — hot. The trick is not to overcook the vegetables. Fry them quickly in their own juices started off with a tablespoon of olive oil and a thimble of tamari sauce.

"Add herbs (your preference) and one finely chopped clove of garlic. Vegetables should include one large onion, one green pepper, chopped spinach, celery, sliced cucumbers, etc."

Chili Con Carne

by Robert Goulet

"My chili has become quite popular among my friends. They have all dedicated themselves to finding the antidote. If you like the chili please drop by the theater and let me hear about it. If your feelings run to the negative side write a nasty letter to Jack Jones."

Serves: 8

Ingredients:

½ cup butter
2 medium onions, chopped
6 shallots, chopped
1 can (7 oz.) green chilies, chopped
2 garlic cloves, minced
3 lbs. chopped sirloin
1 lb. sausage meat
2 cans (16 oz. ea.) kidney beans
1 jar (4 oz.) pimento
3 lbs. tomatoes, chopped

¾ cup celery, chopped
1 sweet red pepper, chopped
1 hot red pepper, chopped
1 bottle (13 oz.) chili sauce
salt to taste
1 tablespoon garlic salt
2 tablespoons pepper
1 tablespoon oregano
4 tablespoons chili powder
2 tablespoons chili sauce for topping

Directions:

Melt butter in skillet; add onions, shallots, chilies and garlic. Saute until soft. Add sirloin and cook until brown.

Brown sausage in separate pan; pour off fat. Add to onion-beef mixture. Put meat mixture into large kettle; add beans, pimento, tomatoes, celery, sweet and hot peppers and chili sauce. Salt to taste.

Bring to boil. Simmer for 2 hours, stirring about every 15 minutes. Correct seasonings. Skim off fat before serving. Add additional chili sauce.

Chicken and Sausage Gumbo

by Ron Guidry

Chicken and sliced smoked sausage cook together for a flavorful "Deep South" style Gumbo.

Serves: 6 to 8

Ingredients:

1 large chicken, cut up
1 cup cooking oil
salt
pepper
paprika
2 cups onions, chopped
1 cup flour
water, about 16 cups
1½ to 2 lbs. smoked
    sausage, sliced

salt
red cayenne pepper
2 teaspoons parsley,
    chopped
2 teaspoons scallions,
    chopped
6 servings cooked rice

Directions:

Brown chicken in oil, slightly. Remove from oil. Sprinkle chicken with salt, pepper, and paprika. Add flour slowly, stirring constantly over medium heat until medium brown. Add onions and cook until soft.

Add water. Mix. Put chicken back in pot and cook slowly until chicken is done, about 45 minutes to 1 hour. Taste for seasoning. Add salt and pepper, if needed. Add cayenne pepper to taste. Add parsley and scallions. Add sausage and cook approximately 15 minutes. (Sausage may be boiled in a separate pan for 10 minutes to remove excess grease.)

Serve in large soup plate over cooked rice.

Lasagne

by Bruce Jenner

A classic recipe with all the ingredients that go together to make Lasagne great!

Serves: 8 to 10
Oven: 350°

Ingredients:

1 lb. ground beef
½ lb. ground pork or pork sausage
1 medium onion, chopped
1 garlic clove, minced
1 can (1 lb.) tomatoes
1 can (15 oz.) tomato sauce
2 tablespoons parsley flakes

2 tablespoons sugar
1 teaspoon salt
3 cups ricotta or cottage cheese
½ cup Parmesan cheese
1 teaspoon oregano
1 tablespoon dried parsley
1½ teaspoons salt
8 oz. lasagne noodles
¾ lb. mozzarella cheese

Directions:

Brown meat, sausage, onion and garlic clove. Drain fat. Add tomatoes, tomato sauce, parsley flakes, sugar, salt and basil. Simmer uncovered about 45 minutes.

Cook lasagne noodles, drain. In a separate bowl, combine ricotta or cottage cheese, Parmesan cheese, (reserving some for the top), parsley flakes, salt and oregano. Blend well. Grate mozzarella and Parmesan (reserving some for the top). Layer ½ noodles in buttered 9x13" pan. Spread with half ricotta mix, mozzarella cheese and meat. Repeat. Sprinkle with reserved Parmesan cheese. Bake uncovered at 350° for 50 to 60 minutes, until brown and bubbly.

Swiss Cheese Potato Casserole

by DeForest Kelley

A helpful hint to all potato lovers: "This dish can be made the day before, refrigerated and baked 15 minutes longer."

Serves: 8
Oven: 350°

Ingredients:

4 whole potatoes (about 3 lbs.)
1½ lbs. Swiss cheese, shredded

½ cup butter
salt, pepper and paprika to taste

Directions:

Boil potatoes in their skins until half-cooked. Chill, preferably overnight. Peel potatoes and grate into a bowl. Place a layer of potatoes in well-buttered 2-quart shallow baking dish. Sprinkle with a layer of cheese. Dot with butter. Sprinkle with salt and pepper, sparingly. Repeat layer and spinkle top with paprika. Bake at 350° for about an hour.

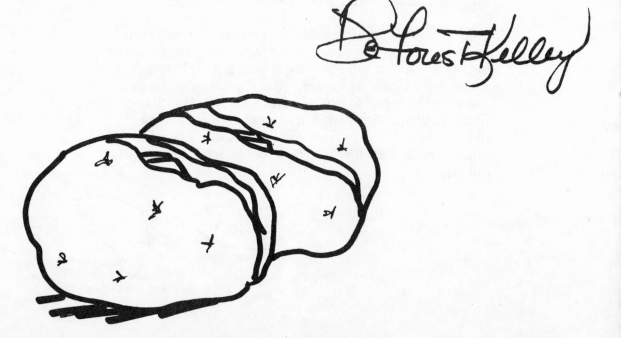

True Old Irish Potato Sandwich
by Gene Kelly

"After first bite of this delicacy you will realize the need for the beer, and will not have to be advised to swallow it in great gulps after each morsel. *Slante!*"

Serves: As many helpings as are left-over.

Ingredients:

- White bread — "the best kind is the cheapest brand one can buy at the store with lots of preservatives and is considered by nutritionists to to be the most unhealthy."
- At least one-day old baked, mashed or boiled potatoes, preferably boiled.
- Onions (sliced) —"... the bigger size and the stronger smell and taste, the better."
- Mustard or mayonnaise (as preferred) ". . . the writer, grown soft in America, prefers mayonnaise."
- Salt —" . . . use plenty, even when suffering the worst cholesterol condition known to man."
- Butter—". . . also ignore high cholesterol count. Do you want a good snack or do you want to be healthy??"
- Beer—". . . Lager-Irish, Dutch and German are superior, but again one must choose according to taste."

Directions:

Butter two sides of bread thickly. Spread on ½" layer of day-old potatoes from the frig. Salt heavily. Apply thin layer of mayonnaise. Cover with onion slices (not too thin), then more mayonnaise on top of the onions and another sprinkle of salt. Add second slice of buttered bread. Be sure to never cut off the crust.

Gene Kelly

Cape Cod Fish Chowder

by Ted Kennedy

Even if you have never walked the beach at Cape Cod, the thought conjures up fleets of fishing boats and favorite foods of the Cape. Enjoy this hearty New England favorite!

Serves: 8

Ingredients:

2 lbs. Haddock
2 oz. salt pork, diced, or
    2 tablespoons
    shortening
2 onions, sliced
1 cup chopped celery
4 large potatoes, diced

1 bay leaf, crumbled
1 qt. milk
2 tablespoons butter or
    margarine
1 teaspoon salt
freshly ground black
    pepper, to taste

Directions:

Simmer Haddock in 2 cups of water for 15 minutes. Drain the reserve broth. Remove bones from the fish.

Saute diced pork until crisp. Remove and set aside. Saute onions in pork fat or shortening until golden brown. Add fish, potatoes, celery, bay leaf, salt, and pepper. Pour fish broth, plus enough boiling water, to make 3 cups liquid.

Simmer for 30 minutes. Add milk and butter and simmer for an additional 5 minutes until well heated. Add pepper to taste.

Ted Kennedy

Spaghetti Sauce

by Jack Klugman

A spaghetti sauce for the most discriminating connoisseur. Features a blend of three meats and lots of garlic!

Yield: 5 to 6 quarts

Ingredients:

⅓ cup olive oil
3 lbs. pork with bone
1 lb. sweet sausage
1 lb. hot sausage
3 cans (28 oz. ea.) whole tomatoes
2 cans (29 oz. ea.) tomato puree
⅔ can (28 oz.) water

1 can (6 oz.) tomato paste
1 can (6 oz.) water
14 garlic cloves, pressed
3 tablespoons salt
1 teaspoon pepper
2 tablespoons fresh oregano
2 tablespoons basil leaves
3 tablespoons parsley

Directions:

Heat oil. Add garlic and brown. Add pork, sweet sausage and hot sausage. Drain.

Place whole tomatoes, tomato puree, tomato paste, and water (both cans) in blender; blend well. Add tomato mixture and seasonings to meat and garlic. Bring to boil.

Cover and simmer at least 2 hours, stirring frequently. Correct seasonings, if necessary.

Jack Klugman

Sour Cream Veal or Beef Loaf

by Janet Leigh

An interesting meat loaf using sour cream and carrots to moisten and add flavor.

Serves: 12
Oven: 350°

Ingredients:

3 lbs. ground veal or very
    lean beef
1 lb. ground pork
½ cup minced onion

4 carrots, ground
1 tablespoon salt
¼ teaspoon pepper
½ cup sour cream

Directions:

Combine veal or beef, pork, onion, carrots, salt, pepper and sour cream. Pack into two 8x4" loaf pans or one large size loaf pan. Bake at 350° for 1½ hours.

Janet Leigh

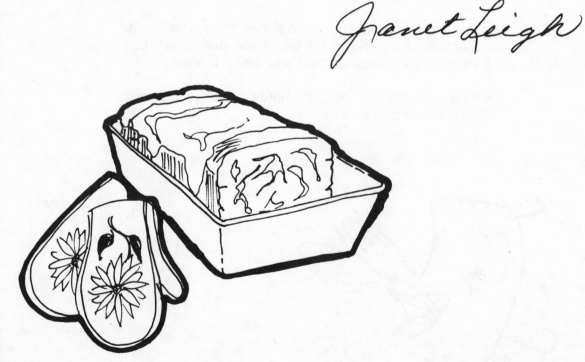

Hamburger Veggie Skillet

by Art Linkletter

A wonderful family supper using "on hand" ingredients.

**Serves: 3 or 4
very hungry
eaters**

Ingredients:

2 lbs. ground round
1 large bell pepper, diced
1 large onion, diced
1 clove of garlic, minced
1 can (8 oz.) water
    chestnuts, coarsely
    chopped

4 stalks of celery, diced
1 can (16 oz.) baby
    tomatoes, chopped
oregano, thyme, salt and
    pepper to taste

Directions:

Brown meat. Add pepper, onion, garlic, water chestnuts, celery, tomatoes and seasonings. Simmer until vegetables are cooked "al dente" (just done). Do not over cook vegetables, just 'til crunchy.

Serve over rice.

Wild Rice Casserole

by Joan Mondale

A casserole dish can be elegant or everyday. This casserole we would describe as elegant and delicious for any dinner party.

Serves: 6 to 8
Oven: 350°

Ingredients:

4 cups boiling water
1 cup uncooked wild rice
1 can mushroom soup
1 can cream of chicken soup
2 small cans mushrooms, drained
2 to 3 beef bouillon cubes in 1 cup water
1 teaspoon salt

1 bay leaf crumbled
¼ teaspoon each: celery salt, garlic salt, pepper (freshly ground), onion salt, and paprika
¾ cup chopped celery
6 tablespoons chopped onion
1½ lbs. lean ground beef
½ cup slivered almonds
½ cup sherry

Directions:

Pour boiling water over rice and let stand 15 minutes. Drain. Place in large casserole adding soups, mushrooms, bouillon and seasonings. Mix gently. Add onions and celery. Brown meat and add.

Sprinkle with almonds and refrigerate. Before baking pour sherry over top. When ready to bake — bake covered for 1½ hours at 350°. (Check at 1 hour.)

114

Mashed Potatoes Army Style

by LeRoy Neiman

"When I was first cook during WWII, mashed potatoes were always a favorite of the troops and of kitchen personnel too, because they were so easily spooned out on the chow line.

The secret was to make them white, moist, and fluffy . . . eye-appealing.

First of all an added joy was knowing that the spuds were lovingly peeled by K.P.'s who were generally given this detail as a traditional punishment.

The potatoes were then classically quartered and in keeping with the words of the mythical 'dieing mess-sergeant,' the potatoes were started out in cold water. All vegetables grown underground, according to the A.R. cooking manual, were started in cold water; all vegetables grown above ground started in warm water.

The potatoes, once well-boiled and drained thoroughly, were mashed, mashed, and mashed, with milk or cream added along the way. Once smooth, a generous chunk of butter is tossed in and pepper added.

Then the secret touch. Stir in a portion of baking powder to make them fluffy . . . not enough to taste but enough to make them white and fluffy . . . 'Army Style'."

French Cheese Sandwich Deluxe

by Kellee Patterson

A marvelous recipe for a yummy baked sandwich. Filled with ham and three cheeses! Perfect for many occasions.

Serves: 4
Oven: 350°

Ingredients:

1 loaf French bread, cut into twelve ½" slices
6 slices of mild Cheddar cheese
6 slices of Monterey Jack cheese
6 thin slices of Danish ham
½ cup Parmesan cheese, grated
3 eggs

1¾ cups milk
3 tablespoons onion, minced
1½ teaspoons prepared mustard
¾ teaspoon salt
⅛ teaspoon pepper
2 teaspoons parsley, minced

Directions:

Trim crust from bread. Arrange half of bread in a greased 9" square or equivalent baking pan.

Layer with slices of Monterey Jack cheese, then slice of ham, then slice of Cheddar. Sprinkle with all but 2 tablespoons of grated Parmesan cheese.

Cover with remaining bread and sprinkle with remaining Parmesan. Beat eggs with milk, onion, mustard, salt, pepper and parsley. Pour over bread. Bake uncovered in 350° oven for 45 minutes or until golden and puffed. Serve promptly.

Kellee Patterson

Beef Stew

by Burt Reynolds

If you don't have a favorite stew recipe, this one is bound to become a favorite! It has just the right blend of flavors to compliment the meat and vegetables.

Serves: 4 to 6
Oven: 325°

Ingredients:

3 slices bacon cut into small pieces
2 lbs. of lean beef, cut into 1″ cubes ("chuck is juicy")
flour (enough to cover meat)
salt and pepper to taste
1 tablespoon of sugar
few dashes MSG
1 onion, chopped
1 clove garlic, minced

1 can (8 oz.) tomato sauce
1 cup beef bouillon or water
1 cup dry burgundy wine
2 carrots, cut up coarsely
2 large potatoes, cut into quarters
2 stalks of celery, cut up coarsely
½ cup fresh whole mushrooms
1 bay leaf (if you like it)
pinch of thyme

Directions:

Cook bacon in a large heavy pot. Salt and pepper beef and dip into flour. Brown in bacon fat, turning often. Add a little oil if needed.

Sprinkle with sugar. Add onion, garlic and brown a little. Add tomato sauce, water or broth, wine, bay leaf, and thyme.

Cover and bake slowly at 325° for about 1½ hours. Add carrots, celery, potatoes and mushrooms. Uncover and cook until meat and vegetables are tender, about another 45 minutes to an hour.

Texas Tacos

by Kyle Rote, Jr.

Now you can make tacos at home that will compare with best restaurants anywhere!

Yields: 10 to 12 tacos

Ingredients:

1 large onion, chopped
cooking oil
1½ to 2 lbs. lean ground
    beef
1 can (16 oz.) whole
    tomatoes, chopped
½ teaspoon salt, or to taste
½ teaspoon pepper, or to
    taste

½ teaspoon cumin
½ teaspoon garlic powder
½ teaspoon chili powder
10 to 12 taco shells
chopped lettuce
chopped tomatoes
shredded cheese

Directions:

Saute onion in oil. Add beef and brown. Drain off excess fat. Add tomatoes. Add spices according to your taste.

Cover; simmer for 2 hours. Stir often. Use this meat mixture in heated taco shells and garnish with chopped lettuce, tomato and cheese. Fills approximately 10 to 12 taco shells.

Tennessee Lasagne

by Dinah Shore

"My version of lasagne is one of those dishes that is most useful when people unexpectedly drop over and you have to substitute several ingredients to make it stre-ee-etch. On one occasion I added cheese. On another, more macaroni.

It's an economical dish, and my usual practice is to make two and put one in the freezer. Then, whenever guests drop in unexpectedly, as they say in commercials, I pop the frozen one in the oven.

What's more, Tennessee Lasagne reheats well, and it's good the second day. Reassemble it in a smaller casserole, sprinkle more cheese over the top, add tomato juice if you need it, and reheat slowly and thoroughly. I've hardly ever had a more accommodating dish."

Serves: 10 to 12
Oven: 350°

Ingredients:

1 medium onion, chopped
2 cloves garlic, minced
1 small bunch of celery, chopped
1 green pepper, cut in broad strips
2 lbs. ground meat (ground chuck or 1 lb. ground chuck and 1 lb. hot Italian sausage)
1 teaspoon salt
½ teaspoon pepper
1 teaspoon chili powder
¼ teaspoon cumin
dash of Worcestershire
¼ teaspoon oregano
6 to 8 whole mushrooms, sliced thin
¾ teaspoon red pepper flakes
2 cans (16 oz. ea.) tomatoes
1 can (8 oz.) tomato sauce
1 lb. sharp Cheddar cheese, cut in cubes
1 pkg. (1 lb.) elbow macaroni, cooked
Parmesan cheese

Directions:

Brown onions and garlic in oil. Add celery and green pepper, cook until soft. Remove from pan. Add meat and brown well. Drain.

CONTINUED —

Tennessee Lasagne

by Dinah Shore

Directions:

Add salt, pepper, chili powder, cumin, Worcestershire, oregano, mushrooms, red pepper flakes, tomatoes and tomato sauce. Add sauteed onion, celery and green pepper. Simmer for 1 hour.

In a greased 9x13″ pan, layer ingredients, beginning with cooked macaroni, cheese cubes, sauce, and very *lightly* sprinkle with red pepper flakes. Repeat procedure ending with sauce. Sprinkle with Parmesan. Bake at 350° for approx. 45 minutes. This can be prepared ahead. Serve with crusty French bread.

Hot and Spicy Japanese Eggplant

by Audrey Meadows Six

"You may use this dish hot as a vegetable side dish. It is excellent with a meat course. You may also use it cold, as an appetizer or relish. It is also delicious!"

Serves: 4 to 6

Ingredients:

5 to 6 medium size eggplants
4 tablespoons soy sauce
4 tablespoons vinegar
2 to 3 tablespoons sugar
1 tablespoon ginger, finely chopped
2 tablespoons green onions, finely chopped, including tops

½ teaspoon chili paste with garlic available in Oriental food stores or gourmet section in supermarket
2 tablespoons peanut oil
2 tablespoons water

Directions:

This recipe must be made with Japanese eggplants which do not have seeds and are very tender. They are much smaller and narrower than regular eggplants.

Cut the eggplant in small cubes, leaving the skin on. Marinate the eggplant cubes in all of the ingredients for approximately 15 to 20 minutes. The longer the eggplant cubes remain in the marinade the hotter the dish will be.

Heat small amount of peanut oil in a frying pan or wok. Remove eggplant from marinade and saute in the hot oil. When partly done, add 2 tablespoons of water. Cover and steam for a few minutes. Add marinade and simmer until reduced to thin gravy.

Audrey Meadows Six

Curried Creamed Spinach

by Robert Stack

"Nice addition to meat, fish or poultry. If done right, your friends will think you've been slaving over the stove for hours."

Serves: 2 to 4

Ingredients:

1 pkg. frozen chopped spinach, thoroughly drained or 1 cup fresh spinach, chopped
1 cup white sauce, homemade or canned

¼ teaspoon curry powder
1 teaspoon Worcestershire sauce
juice of ½ lemon
pinch of garlic salt

Directions:

Cook spinach and drain well.

Add white sauce, curry powder, Worcestershire sauce, lemon juice and garlic salt.

Mix well and stir over low flame.

Chili

by Jean Stapleton

This recipe takes advantage of a convenience food, seasoning mix for chili, to make it easy and delicious.

Yield: approx. 3 to 4 qts.

Ingredients:

2½ lbs. ground round
1 can (8 oz.) mushrooms
2 medium onions, chopped
salt and pepper, to taste
2 pkgs. Schilling seasoning
   mix for chili
1 can (16 oz.) tomato sauce

1 can (16 oz.) tomatoes,
   peeled
1 can (16 oz.) red kidney
   beans, drained
1 cup uncooked spaghetti,
   broken into pieces
water

Directions:

Brown ground round with mushrooms and onions. Drain. Add salt, pepper and Schilling seasoning. Stir well. Add tomato sauce, peeled tomatoes, kidney beans and broken spaghetti. Mix well. Add approximately 1½ cups water. Simmer for 1 hour.

Jean Stapleton

I PARTICIPATE IN SPECIAL OLYMPICS

Favorite Meat Loaf

by Robert Sterling

This meat loaf boasts some surprise flavor ingredients and a sauce that bakes on.

Serves: 6 to 8
Oven: 350°

Ingredients:

1 lb. lean ground beef
½ lb. ground sausage
1 egg, beaten
1 cup bread crumbs, or 4 slices bread soaked in milk
1 medium onion, chopped
1 teaspoon salt
¼ teaspoon pepper
1 to 2 teaspoons curry powder
1 can (8 oz.) tomato sauce, reserve 4 oz.

Sauce:

reserved 4 oz. tomato sauce
2 tablespoons vinegar
2 tablespoons brown sugar
2 tablespoons prepared mustard

Directions:

Mix meats, egg, bread crumbs, onion, salt, pepper, curry powder and ½ can (4 oz.) tomato sauce. Form into loaf and place in greased pan. Mix sauce mixture and pour over loaf. Bake at 350° for 1 hour.

Robert Sterling

Alsatian Stew

by Loretta Swit

An inspired "Old World" layered stew with delicious seasonings that flavor perfectly.

Serves: 6
Oven: 350°

Ingredients:

1 lb. veal stew meat
1 lb. pork stew meat
1 lb. new potatoes sliced
2 medium onions, thinly sliced
⅓ cup parsley, chopped

2 garlic cloves, minced
2 bay leaves
½ bottle or 12 oz. dry white wine (Riesling)
¼ cup butter

Directions:

Cut meat into 1″ chunks. Cut potatoes into ¼″ slices. In a 4 quart pan or Dutch oven, layer the meat, potatoes, onions, parsley and garlic.

Sprinkle pepper and 1 bay leaf on layer. Repeat. Place ¼ cup of butter on top. Pour wine over layers. Cover tightly. Bake at 350° for 1 hour and 45 minutes.

Loretta Swit

HUGGER
A SPECIAL OLYMPIAN AT HEART

125

Bahamian Peas 'n Rice

by Mychal Thompson

"This is the most delicious type of rice in the world. I also think this is the secret to growing tall . . . look at me, I gobbled up this rice every day . . . and grew to 6'10" and to play in the N.B.A."

Serves: 6 to 8

Ingredients:

½ lb. salt pork, thinly sliced
2 tablespoons cooking oil
1 medium onion, finely diced
¼ cup celery, diced finely
1 can (4 oz.) tomato sauce

1 teaspoon pepper
½ teaspoon garlic salt
½ teaspoon thyme leaves
1 can (12 oz.) pigeon peas
1 cup water
2 cups uncooked rice

Directions:

Place salt pork in pot and fry until crisp. Remove salt pork and leave oil in pot. Add 2 tablespoons of cooking oil.

Add onion, celery, tomato sauce, pepper, garlic salt and thyme to cooking oil. Cook on high for about 15 minutes, stirring occasionally, or until onion and celery are tender and mixture boils.

Blend in pigeon peas, including water in can. Add water and bring to a boil. Blend in rice. Cook on medium, covered, for about 30 minutes or until water is absorbed. Stir, from bottom to top, halfway through cooking time. Cover.

When water is absorbed, stir rice again from bottom to top. Reduce heat to low until rice is cooked, thoroughly.

Tip: Black-eyed peas can be substituted for pigeon peas. Can be served with any meat.

Mychal "Bells" Thompson

Chop Suey

by Brad Van Pelt

Here are some special hints for this delicious chop suey "Salt, pepper and soy sauce may be added depending on individual taste. Also, chop suey may be thickened if desired."

Serves: 8 to 10

Ingredients:

2½ lbs. chop suey meat, (pork, beef, veal), cubed
½ teaspoon salt
¼ teaspoon pepper
1 medium onion, chopped
1½ cups celery, diced
1 can (28 oz.) chop suey vegetables, drained
1 can (16 oz.) bean sprouts, drained

2 cans (10 oz. ea.) condensed cream of mushroom soup
1 can (8 oz.) mushrooms, drained
2 teaspoons soy sauce
2 cups water
2 cans (3 oz. ea.) chow mein noodles
cooked rice

Directions:

Brown meat. Add salt, pepper, onion and celery; continue browning to transparent stage. Add chop suey vegetables, bean sprouts, soup, mushrooms, soy sauce and water.

Cook at medium heat for 30 minutes. Reduce heat to simmer for additional 1½ hours, stirring occasionally. Add water if necessary. Serve chop suey over cooked rice and sprinkle chow mein noodles on top.

Brad Van Pelt

California Souffle

by Harry Von Zell

A "do ahead" luncheon or supper dish that contains America's favorite ingredients.

Serves: 8 to 10
Oven: 325°

Ingredients:

8 slices day-old bread
¼ cup butter or margarine
2 cups mushrooms, sliced
1 cup onion, minced
2 cups diced cooked ham
4 cups shredded Cheddar cheese

2 tablespoons flour
8 eggs
2 tablespoons prepared mustard
2 cups half and half
1 teaspoon garlic salt
1 teaspoon salt, or to taste

Directions:

Trim crusts off bread and cut in bite size pieces. Arrange in well-buttered 13x9" baking dish. Heat butter in skillet and saute mushrooms and onion about 5 minutes.

Spoon evenly over bread cubes. Top with ham. Combine cheese with flour and sprinkle over ham. Beat eggs with mustard, half and half, garlic salt and salt. Pour into dish.

Cover; refrigerate at least 4 hours or overnight. Bake uncovered at 325° for 1 hour, or until puffed and lightly browned.

Harry Von Zell

SEVEN

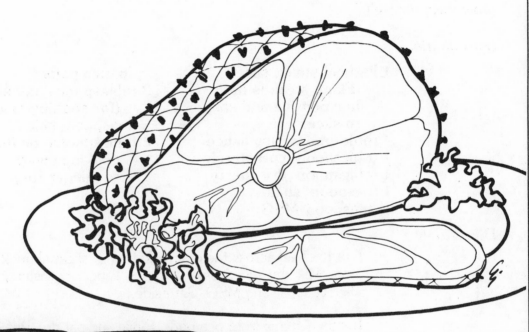

Meat

Beef with Pea Pods (Snow Peas)

by Steve Allen

"This is a wonderful dish to be served at the family table as well as at a party. Although the pea pods are obtainable only at Chinese groceries, it is worth the trouble to buy them fresh. If you have a vegetable garden, you can grow them yourself."

Serves: 4 to 6

Ingredients:

1 lb. beef steak, sliced
   (Flank steak is fairly
   inexpensive and easy
   to slice)
4 tablespoons soy sauce
1 tablespoon cornstarch
1 tablespoon dry sherry
1 teaspoon sugar
¼ teaspoon MSG

¼ lb. pea pods
2 tablespoons cooking oil
   (for cooking peas)
½ teaspoon salt
2 tablespoons oil (for
   cooking meat)
1 slice ginger root

Directions:

Cut the beef across the grain into thin ¼" slices about 2" long. Mix the sliced beef with soy sauce, cornstarch, sherry, sugar and MSG. Set aside.

Remove stems from pea pods. Rinse and pat dry. Put 2 tablespoons of oil in skillet over high flame. Add salt first and then the pea pods, stirring constantly until the pods turn a darker green (less than 1 minute). Remove the pods and spread out on a plate.

In the same skillet add the remaining 2 tablespoons of oil and ginger root. Stir in the beef mixture and turn constantly until beef is almost cooked (not over 2 minutes). Add pea pods and mix thoroughly. For crispness do not overcook.

Serve immediately. When pea pods are inadequate or unobtainable, substitute sliced bamboo shoots or mushrooms (black or fresh) or sliced tender celery.

Beef Bourguignon (Beef in Burgundy Sauce)

by Robby Benson

A dinner party entree that is so easy to put together, can be prepared ahead and is sure to get raves.

Serves: 6
Oven: 350°
or simmer

Ingredients:

3 lbs. of lean beef chuck, cut in 1-inch cubes
1 can (10½ oz.) condensed consomme
1 cup V-8 juice
1 cup burgundy wine
½ cup brown sugar, firmly packed

1 can (10½ oz.) condensed onion soup
½ teaspoon garlic powder
½ teaspoon oregano
½ teaspoon celery salt
2 bay leaves
⅓ cup water
3 tablespoons cornstarch

Directions:

In large saucepan, combine all ingredients except water and cornstarch. Cover and simmer slowly until meat is tender, about 2 hours. Stir occasionally, or . . . bake in Dutch oven, covered at 350° for approximately 2 hours.

Combine water and cornstarch. Mix until smooth. Add to hot stew. Cook until sauce thickens. Serve over rice.

SPECIAL OLYMPICS VOLUNTEER

Pernil (Roast Pork from Puerto Rico)

by Erik Estrada

"Top off this Puerto Rican style roast pork with 'Moros y Cristianos' (rice and black beans), 'Platanos Fritos' (fried plantains or bananas) or 'Ensalada de cebolla y tomate' (sliced red onions and tomato salad with olive oil and parsley)."

Serves: 6 to 8
Oven: 350°

Ingredients:

1 large pork loin, 3 to 5 lbs.
1 lemon
1 large clove garlic (or garlic powder)
1 bay leaf
pinch of sage, rosemary, tarragon or thyme, if desired

salt and pepper, to taste
paprika and onion salt, to taste
¼ cup flour
½ cup red wine

Directions:

Preheat oven to 450°. Rub meat liberally with lemon juice, garlic, bay leaf, sage, rosemary, tarragon and thyme. Sprinkle with salt, pepper, onion salt, paprika and flour.

Place roast in pan in oven, fat side up. Lower heat immediately to 350°. Cook, uncovered, about 35 minutes per pound or until internal temperature is 185°. After roast is in oven for about an hour, baste with wine.

Erik Estrada

Chuck Roast With Vegetables

by Betty Ford

Is there an American anywhere who doesn't count among his or her favorite dishes a beef roast with vegetables? A former first lady shares her recipe!

Serves: 6
Oven: 350°

Ingredients:

6 lbs. boneless beef chuck, oven ready
salt and black pepper
flour
6 boiled potatoes, peeled and cut in half
2 tablespoons corn oil

12 small onions, peeled
6 medium-sized white turnips, peeled and cut in half
12 small carrots, peeled
2 cups beef bouillon

Directions:

Season meat with salt and pepper. Then roll the meat in the flour to coat all sides.

Brown the meat in 2 tablespoons corn oil in an iron skillet. When it is well browned, transfer the meat to a roasting pan, adding 1 cup of beef bouillon and cover. Simmer for 1½ hours in oven, basting the meat with the bouillon from time to time.

Surround the chuck roast with all the vegetables. Salt the vegetables and pour the second cup of bouillon over the vegetables. Again cover and simmer for another hour or until tender.

Remove the meat from the pan to a platter and let rest for 15 minutes. Keep the vegetables warm.

Slice the meat on a cutting board and arrange the slices on the serving platter. Arrange the vegetables around the meat.

Bring the gravy to a boil. Pour it into a small pot. Again bring it to a boil. Remove from the heat and remove the fat from the gravy by placing a paper towel on the top of the gravy. (The fat will be absorbed by the paper.) Serve the hot gravy separately.

Betty Ford

Baked Pork Roman Style

by Linda Gary

This hearty one-dish meal teams all the best-loved flavors of Italian cooking with pork chops.

Serves: 6 to 8
Oven: 350°

Ingredients:

12 center-cut pork chops, thinly sliced
Lawrys seasoned salt
Lawrys seasoned pepper
3 green peppers
1 pkg. (8 oz.) mozzarella cheese
1 pkg. (16 oz.) elbow macaroni or mostaccioli or rigatoni, cooked and drained

3 cloves garlic, minced
1 large can (28 oz.) peeled tomatoes
1 small can (8 oz.) tomato sauce
1 teaspoon dried oregano (2 teaspoons, if fresh)
1 teaspoon dried basil (2 teaspoons, if fresh)

Directions:

Brown pork chops in small amount of oil. Season with Lawrys salt and pepper. Transfer chops to a 9x13" pan.

Par boil green peppers about 5 minutes. Cut peppers into 2x1" pieces and put one slice on top of each chop. Divide cheese and place one slice on top of chop and green pepper.

To make sauce, brown 3 cloves of garlic in a little oil. Add tomatoes and tomato sauce. Add oregano, basil and a pinch of Lawrys salt and pepper. Cook for 20 minutes.

Add sauce to chops and bake covered for 1 hour at 350°. Remove chops from pan and mix the cooked macaroni with the sauce. Serve the chops on top of the macaroni.

Calf's Liver Avec Moutarde
by Graham Jarvis

"This is one of our most favorite dishes. It hardly tastes of liver at all because the sauce is so good and so concealing at the same time."

Serves: 4

Ingredients:

1 lb. calf's liver or beef liver
½ cup wheat germ
½ teaspoon salt
½ teaspoon pepper
2 tablespoons butter

1 tablespoon oil
½ cup chicken broth
½ cup whipping cream
2 tablespoons Dijon-style mustard
parsley sprigs, if desired

Directions:

Roll liver in wheat germ, salt and pepper. Melt butter and oil until hot. Saute liver for about 3 minutes on each side. If using beef liver, saute for about 5 minutes on each side.

Remove liver to hot platter. Add broth and boil rapidly until liquid is reduced to one-half. Turn to low heat and slowly add cream, stirring constantly. Add mustard and mix well. Pour sauce over meat and serve. Add parsley sprigs, if desired.

Graham Jarvis

135

Scallopinne Presto

by Steven T. Johnson

"Sing one chorus of *Volare* and serve."

Serves: 2

Ingredients:

6 pieces veal scallopine
   (⅛ to ¼" thick — about
   2 to 4" wide)
salt
2 tablespoons flour

oregano, if desired
¼ cup butter
½ cup Italian white wine
   (Soave Bolla — the
   drier the better)

Directions:

Lightly flour veal. Melt butter on low heat. Add wine bit by bit until sauce is a creamy white-yellow. Fry veal in a separate pan until golden brown around the edges. Do not overcook.

Remove veal from pan and pour sauce over meat. Lightly salt and crush a bit of oregano over dish if you desire.

Steven T. Johnson

SPECIAL OLYMPICS VOLUNTEER

A La Flamande (A Flemish Pork)

by Ron Masak

"This is a fun recipe to experiment with using your own favorite vegetables. Different brands of beer change the taste slightly."

Serves: 6 to 8

Ingredients:

3 tablespoons butter
2½ lbs. pork shoulder, diced
salt and pepper to taste
3 cups beer
½ cup boiling water
1 teaspoon dried crushed rosemary
1 jar (16 oz.) pearl onions

2 cups bouillon
2 pkgs. frozen brussel sprouts, thawed
2 cups carrots, sliced, partially cooked
2 cups potatoes, sliced, partially cooked
¼ cup all purpose flour
3 tablespoons water

Directions:

Melt butter in a large kettle and brown meat. Add salt, pepper, beer, water and rosemary. Simmer covered for 45 minutes. Add onions. Cover and simmer for 30 minutes.

Add bouillon, brussel sprouts, potatoes, and carrots and simmer for 25 minutes.

Blend flour and water to make paste. Gradually stir into beef and vegetable mixture. Stir until thickened.

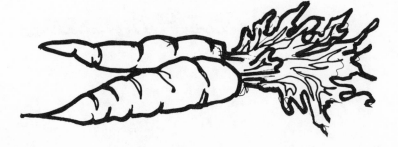

137

Marinade for Chicken, Beef and Pork

by Walter Mondale

Vice President Walter Mondale's favorite summer supper includes barbecued chicken, grilled corn on the cob, wild rice, green salad with mustard vinaigrette dressing, sliced tomatoes and fresh summer fruits.

Serves: 8

Ingredients:

1 quart pineapple juice	6 cloves garlic, crushed
1 cup soy sauce	2/3 teaspoon aniseed
2/3 cup white wine	1 cup brown sugar
juice of 2 lemons	1 1/3 teaspoons salt
2" piece fresh ginger, crushed	1/3 teaspoon black pepper
	2 chickens, quartered

Directions:

Combine liquid ingredients in wide bowl or pan. Tie ginger, garlic and aniseed in cheesecloth bag; drop into bowl. Add brown sugar, salt and pepper, stir. Add chicken pieces. Refrigerate several hours or (preferably) overnight. Remove chicken from marinade. Grill about 6" from hot coals, turning to glaze all sides and basting with marinade, about 45 minutes.

Any leftovers are excellent cold. Refrigerate leftover marinade to use again (keeps at least 2 weeks).

Walter F. Mondale

Stuffed Veal Shoulder

by Bob Newhart

The delicate flavor of roast veal is enhanced by a flavorful stuffing and roasting on vegetables with a wine sauce.

Serves: 8 to 10
Oven: 425°

Ingredients:

5 lb. veal roast
6 tablespoons butter
1 small onion, chopped
¾ cup celery, chopped fine with leaves
2 garlic cloves, crushed
6 tablespoons chopped parsley
¾ teaspoon salt and pepper to taste
¾ lb. mushrooms, chopped
1½ teaspoons dried rosemary
3 cups bread crumbs

2 egg yolks
4½ tablespoons heavy cream
3 tablespoons chopped parsley
1 bay leaf
3 celery stalks, coarsely chopped
3 carrots, coarsely chopped
1 small onion, coarsely chopped
½ cup chicken broth
½ cup red wine
3 tablespoons tomato paste

Directions:

Melt butter and add onion, celery and garlic. Cook until transparent. Add parsley, salt, pepper, mushrooms and rosemary. Cook about 2 minutes. Combine bread crumbs, egg yolks and cream and add to above mixture. Mix well.

Lay meat skin side down, season with salt, pepper and garlic salt. Spread with stuffing. Roll and tie. Season and butter outside of roast.

Place parsley, bay leaf, onions, carrots and celery in pan or Dutch oven. Place meat on vegetables. Roast 15 minutes at 425° Reduce oven to 350°.

Mix together broth, wine and tomato paste. Pour over roast. Cover and bake 2 hours. Baste frequently. Remove cover and bake and additional 15 minutes.

Bob Newhart

Saucey Pigs

Jane says, "It sounds a little crazy, but it is so good . . . believe it or not! This is good as an extra dish to accompany meats."

Serves: 6 to 8
Oven: 350°

Ingredients:

2 to 3 lbs. pork link
   sausage
6 to 8 apples, peeled and
   sliced

1½ cups brown sugar
1 bottle (14 oz.) catsup
dash of cinnamon

Directions:

Brown sausage links. Drain. Layer in a 9x13" pan; sausage, apples, brown sugar and catsup. Sprinkle lightly with cinnamon. Bake at 350° for 1½ hours.

Wheel O' Fortune Tenderloin

by Susan Stafford

Special flavors for a special meat that "stir fries" in a Wok or skillet.

Serves: 2 to 4

Ingredients:

1 lb. filet mignon, cut ½"
    thick, 1½" long and 1"
    wide
4 tablespoons hoisin sauce
½ tablespoon salt
1 tablespoon brandy

1 egg white
1 tablespoon cornstarch
1 tablespoon peanut oil
1½ tablespoons peanut oil
    for frying

Directions:

Mix sauce, salt, brandy, egg whites, cornstarch and 1 tablespoon peanut oil. Add strips of meat and marinate for 4 hours.

Preheat wok or skillet. Fry beef in 1½ tablespoons of oil for about 1 minute on each side.

EIGHT

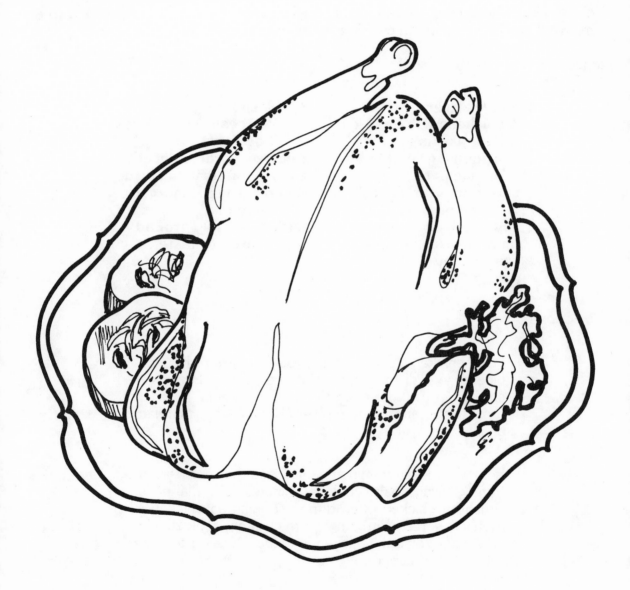

Poultry

Barbecued-Honey-Orange Chicken

by Claude Akins

This delicious "honey and citrus sauced" chicken is so versatile it can be prepared on a grill or in the oven.

Serves: 6 to 8

Ingredients:

2 broiler-fryer chickens (3 lbs. ea.), cut into quarters
2 teaspoons grated fresh orange peel
1 teaspoon grated fresh lemon peel
1 cup fresh orange juice
⅓ cup fresh lemon juice
½ cup honey

2 tablespoons Worcestershire sauce, if desired
2 cloves garlic, minced
1 teaspoon dry mustard
½ cup butter or margarine, melted
salt and freshly ground pepper, to taste

Directions:

Place chicken pieces in plastic bag or glass dish. Combine all ingredients except salt and pepper. Pour over chicken in bag; twist bag to close. Marinate 2 hours at room temperature, turning every 30 minutes to marinate on all sides.

Remove chicken from marinade. Place chicken on grill 6" from glowing coals; cook 20 minutes. Stir marinade. Brush on chicken often during cooking so chicken is evenly flavored. With tongs, turn chicken, cook 20 minutes longer or until chicken is tender. Season to taste with salt and pepper.

Reduce sauce by cooking over medium heat, stirring constantly. Spoon sauce over chicken.

144

CONTINUED —

Barbecued-Honey-Orange Chicken

by Claude Akins

Afterthoughts:

"Recipe works equally well oven-baked indoors. Marinate chicken as directed. Place chicken skin side down in ovenproof baking dish. Brush lavishly with marinade.

Bake in 375° oven for 35 minutes, turn, and continue baking for 35 minutes. Baste often. Recipe works well on a small whole turkey or large drumsticks, duck or rolled pork loin roast."

Claude Akins

Pan-Fried Chicken Kiev

by Alison Arngrim

Alison's new twist on the favorite Chicken Kiev gives a buttery and savory dish.

Serves: 4

Ingredients:

4 large, whole chicken breasts, boned, skinned and split
salt to taste
½ cup butter or margarine, softened
½ cup onion, finely chopped
½ cup parsley, finely chopped

1 egg
1 tablespoon milk
1 tablespoon water
¼ cup butter or margarine
¼ cup flour
1 cup crushed dry herb stuffing

Directions:

Cover chicken with waxed paper and pound with wooden mallet (or rolling pin) until each breast is ¼" thick. Sprinkle with salt. Cream ½ cup butter and add onion and parsley. Divide creamed mixture into 8 portions and spread a portion at one end of each breast. Roll up the chicken pieces, tuck in sides and secure with a toothpick (no string!).

Combine egg, milk and water; beat well. Dust each roll with flour. Dip into egg mixture and roll in stuffing mix. Chill 1 hour.

Fry in hot butter, turning rolls to brown evenly. Drain on paper towel.

Italian Polenta with Chicken and Gravy

by Dick Balduzzi

An old world Italian chicken dish made easy with instant polenta.

Serves: 6

Ingredients:

½ cup olive oil
1 small onion, chopped
1 clove garlic, minced
6 medium chicken legs
4 large chicken breasts, cut in quarters
1 can (8 oz.) mushroom stems and pieces
1 cup white chablis wine
1 slice lemon, cut in quarters

1 pinch sage
1 pinch parsley
1 pinch rosemary
3 cans (14½ oz.) chicken broth
1 tablespoon tomato paste
3 tablespoons flour
2 cups instant polenta

Directions:

CHICKEN AND GRAVY:

In large frying pan, heat oil. Add onion, garlic and saute. Add chicken and brown. Salt and pepper chicken. Add mushrooms, wine, lemon, sage, parsley and rosemary. Cook for 15 minutes over medium heat, turning chicken.

Add one can of chicken broth every 15 minutes. Lower heat and add tomato paste, mixing well. Simmer about 1½ hours until chicken is tender. To make gravy, add flour to hot sauce.

POLENTA:

Use large, deep dish sauce pan. Bring 7 cups of water to boil. Add pinch of salt. Pour in two cups of instant Polenta. Stir constantly with wooden spoon for about 5 minutes.

Pour into a platter in cake-like fashion. Let set a few minutes. Slice and serve with chicken and gravy.

Dick Balduzzi

Chicken with Marinade

by Bob Beattie

A delicious and attractive marinade adds flavor before and during grilling. Thickened with honey added, it turns into a sauce at serving time.

Serves: 4

Ingredients:

½ cup green onion, chopped
½ cup sherry
¼ cup soy sauce
¼ cup water
¼ cup cooking oil

1 teaspoon fresh ginger root, grated
8 chicken breasts, boned and skinned
2 teaspoons cornstarch
1 tablespoon honey

Directions:

Combine green onion, sherry, soy sauce, water, oil and ginger root. Pour over chicken in a 9x13″ pan. Cover and refrigerate 5 hours or overnight, turning chicken several times. Drain chicken, reserving marinade.

Grill over medium coals for 20 minutes, brushing occasionally with marinade. Turn pieces and continue grilling for another 20 minutes or till done.

Add water to remaining marinade, if necessary, to make 1 cup liquid. In saucepan, combine the 1 cup marinade and the cornstarch. Add honey, cooking and stirring until the mixture is thickened and bubbly. Serve sauce with the chicken.

Sweet and Sour Chicken

by Jill Kinmont Boothe

Everybody's favorite chicken bakes up moist and pungent with a flavorful sauce.

Serves: 4
Oven: 325°

Ingredients:

1 medium fryer, cut up
½ cup   wine vinegar
½ cup   soy sauce
⅓ cup   honey
¾ cup   catsup

2 cloves garlic, minced
1 teaspoon prepared
        mustard
salt and pepper to taste

Directions:

Wash and dry fryer. Sprinkle with salt and pepper. Put in 2 quart casserole or 9x13" pan. Combine remaining ingredients and pour over chicken.

Cover and bake at 325° for 2 hours or until very tender. Turn and baste frequently while baking.

Jill Kinmont Boothe

Peking Duck and Wild Life Rice

by Suzy Chaffee

Roast duckling in its most gourmet form with special touches from Chinese cuisine.

Add the delicious rice casserole! It's the perfect accompaniment for any meat or poultry dish also.

Serves: 6
Oven: 375°

PEKING DUCK:

Ingredients:

¼ cup honey
4 slices fresh ginger root, peeled (1" wide, ⅛" thick)
2 scallions, including tops, cut into 2" lengths

1 duckling (5 lb.), washed and dried
12 scallions
mandarin pancakes and plum sauce from Chinese market

Directions:

In 12" wok or large flameproof casserole, combine 6 cups water, honey, ginger root and scallions. Bring to boil over high heat.

Tie length of white cord (20") around neck or wings of duck. Lower into boiling liquid. With string in one hand and large spoon in other, turn duck from side to side until all skin is moistened.

Remove duck (discarding liquid); let dry. (Suzy hurries process by using a hair blower.)

Preheat oven to 375°. Place duck, breast side up on rack in roasting pan. Pour 1" water into pan; roast uncovered for 1 hour. Pour off excess fat.

Lower heat to 300°; roast breast down for 30 minutes. Raise heat to 375°; roast breast up 30 minutes longer to desired crispness and mahogany color.

For fancy scallion brushes: Cut scallions into 3" lengths, trim off roots. Standing each scallion on end, make 4 intersecting cuts 1" deep into white part. If desired, place in ice water in refrigerator until cut apart curls into brush-like fans.

CONTINUED —

Peking Duck and Wild Life Rice

by Suzy Chaffee

To serve: Remove skin from duck in pieces and reserve; slice meat. Arrange meat on platter; with skin and scallion brushes. Set duck sauce on plate with pancakes around it.

Guests fill heated pancakes with piece of duck meat and skin; then brush with scallion dipped in plum sauce; fold pancake over and eat.

WILD LIFE RICE:

Serves: 6

Ingredients:

½ cup wild rice
½ cup brown rice
chicken broth (substitute for water)
1 medium onion, chopped
4 tablespoons butter or margarine

1 can (8 oz.) water chestnuts, sliced
½ lb. snow peas (fresh, if possible)
½ lb. fresh mushrooms, sliced

Directions:

Cook wild and brown rice following label directions, substituting chicken broth for water.

Saute onion in butter. Add water chestnuts, snow peas and mushrooms. Gently stir and heat. Add cooked rice to mixture and toss.

Simmer until hot. Also delicious reheated.

Suzy

Chicken Cannelloni

by Phil Donahue

"Chicken breasts take only minutes to cook, make delicious eating, and you can get them ready for the pan hours ahead of serving time. Accompany these fragrant morsels simply with buttered rice or good French bread, and a chilled bottle of rosé wine. This is a recipe from the famous Julia Child. She shared it with me on my show. I enjoy preparing this chicken recipe myself."

Serves: 4

Ingredients:

4 boned and skinned chicken-breast halves
salt and pepper
2 tablespoons Dijon-style prepared mustard
1 teaspoon herb mixture, such as Provencal or Italian seasoning
1 pkg. (8 oz.) sliced Mozzarella cheese
1 cup flour in a plate
2 to 3 tablespoons olive oil or fresh peanut oil

2 tablespoons minced shallots or scallions
optional: 1 clove minced or puréed fresh garlic
1 cup sliced fresh mushrooms
2 fresh ripe red tomatoes, peeled, seeded, juiced, and chopped (or 1 cup pulp from canned peeled Italian plum tomatoes, drained, and sieved to remove seeds)

Directions:

Open out the boned and skinned chicken breasts (meaning, lift inner flap of breast meat from center, and fold it outward, to extend breast meat). One at a time, pound breasts between 2 sheets of wax paper to flatten and enlarge them, and lay them on your work surface. Season top sides lightly with salt and pepper.

With a rubber spatula, spread a half tablespoon of mustard over the topside of each chicken breast, and sprinkle lightly with the herb mixture. Arrange a slice of Mozzarella on each, and roll up breast from one of its short sides, making a tight, neat package, and pressing the meat in place with your fingers, as necessary. (May be prepared ahead, covered, and refrigerated.) Just before cooking, season lightly with salt and pepper, roll in flour and shake off excess.

152

CONTINUED —

Chicken Cannelloni

by Phil Donahue

Choose a heavy frying pan (no-stick suggested) just large enough to hold chicken easily in one layer. Film with 1/16" of oil and heat to very hot but not smoking. Add the chicken breasts, and sauté, turning several times, for 6 to 8 minutes, regulating heat so chicken browns nicely without burning. Chicken is done when just springy rather than squashy to the touch. Remove chicken to a side dish.

Add the minced shallots or scallions and optional garlic to the pan, cook for a few seconds, then add the mushrooms. Sauté for 2 minutes, and stir in the tomato. Saute, shaking and tossing, for 2 minutes more, then season with salt and pepper, and a sprinkling of herbs to taste. Return chicken to pan and boil rapidly, basting the chicken until the sauce has thickened lightly. Carefully correct seasoning, sprinkle on a tablespoon of fresh parsley, and serve.

Roast Cornish Hens with Turkish Pilaf

by Farrah Fawcett

Farrah Fawcett shares her easy, tarragon and garlic flavored game hens. Turkish Pilaf is perfect with them.

Serves: 4 to 6
Oven: 450°

CORNISH HENS

Ingredients:

4 to 6 hens, washed and
   drained
¾ cup butter
¾ cup dry white wine
5 to 7 tablespoons dry
   tarragon leaves

4 to 6 cloves garlic,
   skinned
garlic salt
2 tablespoons flour

Directions:

Basting sauce: Melt butter, stir in white wine and one tablespoon tarragon.

Sprinkle a slight tablespoon of tarragon inside each hen. Also place one small garlic clove inside each hen. Refrigerate one hour before cooking.

Preheat oven to 450°. Place hens in shallow baking dish. Bake for 5 minutes. Reduce oven temperature to 350° and bake for approximately one hour, basting with sauce at 20 minute intervals until brown and done. Serve on warm platter with Turkish Pilaf.

Gravy: Dissolve flour in one cup of water. Stir in drippings of pan and heat until thickened.

CONTINUED —

Roast Cornish Hens with Turkish Pilaf

by Farrah Fawcett

TURKISH PILAF   Serves: 6 to 8

Ingredients:

2 cups cracked wheat
2 cans (13¾ oz. ea.)
    chicken broth
¼ cup butter or margarine

pepper to taste
1 can chow mein noodles,
    crushed, if desired

Directions:

Combine wheat and broth. Cover and bring to boil. Simmer 20 minutes. Remove and let stand 10 to 12 minutes until liquid is absorbed. Add butter and pepper and toss gently.

Farrah

HUGGER
A SPECIAL OLYMPIAN AT HEART

Lo-Cal Chicken

by Rhonda Fleming

What's a better combination than low calorie and easy to prepare? This chicken recipe is delicious and fits both descriptions!

Serves: 4
Oven: 400°

Ingredients:

1 broiler-fryer chicken
fresh lemon
1 teaspoon pepper
1½ teaspoons oregano
1 can (16 oz.) stewed
   tomatoes

1 envelope (1¼ oz.) dry
   onion soup mix
½ cup chopped green
   pepper
2 tablespoons chopped
   onion

Directions:

Squeeze lemon into a dish. Dip chicken in juice and sprinkle with pepper and oregano. Place in a 9x13″ pan and brown for 10 minutes on each side in a 400° oven.

Mix stewed tomatoes, onion soup, green peppers and onions. Pour over the chicken and reduce oven temperature to 350°. Bake about 45 minutes to 1 hour until tender.

Chicken Hawaiian

by Steve Garvey

Barbecue sauce and pineapple combine to make the chicken breasts deliciously different.

Serves: 4
Oven: 400°

Ingredients:

4 whole chicken breasts
1 bottle (18 oz.) of barbecue sauce (your preference)

⅓ cup melted butter
1 can (15¼ oz.) chunk style pineapple, drained

Directions:

Lightly baste chicken breasts with butter. Place chicken in a 9x13" pan and bake uncovered at 400° for 20 minutes. Cover and bake for 30 minutes. Add barbecue sauce and pineapple. Bake uncovered for approximately 10 minutes.

Chicken Soy

by Monty Hall

Cantonese-style flavors highlight this easy oven Chicken Dish.

Serves: 6 to 8
Oven: 300°

Ingredients:

2 frying chickens, cut up
1/3 cup soy sauce
2/3 cup brown sugar
water
3 tablespoons
    Worcestershire sauce

2 to 4 tablespoons
    powdered ginger
2 cloves garlic, minced
garlic powder

Directions:

Combine soy sauce, brown sugar, Worcestershire sauce. Add enough water to make two cups of syrup.

Cover chicken with powdered ginger, garlic powder and minced garlic cloves.

Place in baking dish and bake for 1 hour at 300°, turning pieces. Pour syrup over chicken and bake another hour at same temperature. Turn and baste often.

Serve on a bed of rice.

Creamed Chicken

by Rose Kennedy

The matriarch of a famous American family shares her chicken dish. Enjoy serving it on patty shells, rice or toast points. It could also be added to a cream sauce with mushrooms, favorite vegetables and a note of sherry.

Serves: 4

Ingredients:

1 chicken
1 teaspoon butter
milk

salt, to taste
pepper, to taste

Directions:

Boil or roast the chicken. Remove skin and bones. Put fowl in grinder. Place butter in a pan. Add chicken and a little milk to get the desired consistency. Add salt and pepper to taste.

Rose Fitzgerald Kennedy

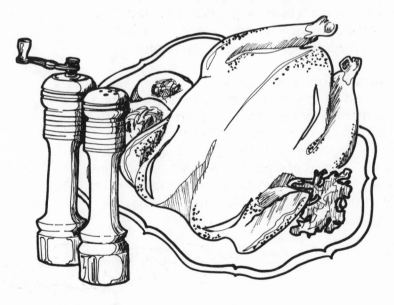

Oven Barbecued Chicken

by Stepfanie Kramer

A special "homemade" barbecue sauce adds a super flavor to this easy oven baked chicken.

Serves: 4 to 6
Oven: 350°

Ingredients:

2 teaspoons salt
¼ teaspoon pepper
2 cans (8 oz. ea.) tomato
     sauce
¼ teaspoon cayenne
     pepper
¼ teaspoon dry mustard
1 bay leaf
4 tablespoons
     Worcestershire sauce

¾ cup apple cider vinegar
10 cloves of garlic, minced
3 tablespoons butter
2 fryers (2½ to 3 lbs. ea.),
     halved
2 medium onions, thinly
     sliced

Directions:

Early in the day:
Make barbecue sauce by combining in a saucepan, salt, pepper, tomato sauce, cayenne pepper, mustard, bay leaf, Worcestershire sauce, vinegar, garlic and butter. Simmer, uncovered, for 10 minutes. Refrigerate.

About 3 hours before serving:
Place chicken and 2 cups of water in a covered pot. Bring to a boil. Simmer 1½ hours. Preheat oven to 350°. Remove skin from chicken. Arrange chicken in a 9x13" pan. Arrange onions on chicken, tucking a few slices under wings and legs. Pour in enough hot water to cover the bottom of the pan, no more. Pour barbecue sauce over chicken. Bake uncovered for 1 to 1½ hours, basting every 15 minutes with sauce in pan.

Stepfanie Kramer

Alabama Chicken

by George Lindsey

This recipe has a special combination of sage, honey and barbecue sauce in the marinade and the basting sauce — Yum Yum!

Serves: 6 to 8
Oven: 300°

Ingredients:

4 chicken breasts
6 thighs
4 legs
1 tablespoon sage

1 cup honey
1 bottle (8 oz.) bar-b-q sauce, any brand

Directions:

Place chicken in a 9x13″ covered pan and bake at 300° for 45 minutes. Drain liquid from pan.

Combine the sage, honey and bar-b-q sauce. Mix well. Cover the chicken with mixture and let stand 3 to 6 hours.

Remove chicken from pan and place on charcoal grill. Turn about every minute so chicken will not burn (honey burns easily). Use remaining bar-b-q marinade, baste chicken while on grill. Cook until tender, usually 15 to 30 minutes.

George Lindsey

Special Turkey Dressing

by Ed McMahon

What makes the traditional Holiday "bird" different? Why the dressing, of course, and this one will be a winner at your Holiday dinners or any time.

Serves: about 20

Ingredients:

1 turkey (about 14 lbs.)
1 pkg. (16 oz.) bread stuffing mix
8 oz. corn bread stuffing
½ cup butter
1 cup celery, chopped
1 cup onion, chopped
1 cup fresh mushrooms, chopped
3 oz. walnuts or pecans, chopped
1 lb. Jone's Country sausage, cooked, crumbled and cooled

1 can (16 oz.) applesauce
1 can (8 oz.) crushed pineapple
6 oz. orange marmalade
1 tablespoon sage
1½ cups brandy (Ed uses ½ bottle) or 1½ cups water
¼ cup melted butter

Directions:

In a large bowl, mix together bread and corn bread stuffings. Saute onion, celery, and mushrooms in ½ cup of butter.

Add cooled mixture to stuffing mixture. Add nuts, cooked sausage, applesauce, pineapple, marmalade, sage, brandy or water and melted butter.

Stuff bird.

Brown Rice and Chicken

by Jan Murray

An attractive and delicious one-dish meal combines chicken, rice and vegetables.

Serves: 6
Oven: 350°

Ingredients:

1 whole chicken breast
   (about ½ lb.)
1 cup brown rice
½ cup wild rice
½ cup vegetable gravy
1 cup fresh or defrosted
   frozen peas

1 tablespoon vegetable
   powder
½ cup chopped fresh
   parsley
2 tablespoons chopped
   pimento

Directions:

Skin chicken. Remove meat from bones and cut into ½" cubes. Teflon fry until pieces stay separate and turn white.

Rinse rice. In a large pot, combine rice and 3 cups of water. Bring to a boil and stir once. Add all other ingredients to rice and water.

Pour into a 3-quart casserole dish. Cover and bake at 350° for 1 hour.

I PARTICIPATE IN SPECIAL OLYMPICS

163

Chicken Cacciatore with Artichokes

by Madlyn Rhue

"Serve with rice or pasta. If you are watching your diet, cut out the salt and MSG and double the garlic. Pass on the sherry. I use skinned, boneless breasts and if you want dark meat, I would use only the thighs."

Serves: 4 to 6
Oven: 350°

Ingredients:

1 jar (6 oz.) marinated
    artichoke hearts
2 tablespoons oil
1 broiler-fryer, (2½ to 3
    lbs.), cut up
flour
1 can (16 oz.) tomatoes
2 cloves garlic, minced

1¼ teaspoons salt
1 teaspoon MSG
½ teaspoon oregano
½ teaspoon basil
½ teaspoon pepper
1 cup mushrooms, sliced
minced parsley
½ cup dry sherry, if desired

Directions:

Drain artichoke hearts. Combine the artichoke liquid with the oil in skillet. Heat until almost sizzling. Coat chicken with flour. Add to hot oil and brown on all sides. Place chicken in a large casserole.

Mix tomatoes, garlic, salt, MSG, oregano, basil, pepper and mushrooms. Pour sauce over chicken.

Cover and bake at 350° for 1 hour or until chicken is tender. Add sherry and artichokes and bake 10 minutes longer. Garnish with parsley.

Madlyn Rhue

Chicken or Turkey Divan

by Mickey Stanley

This is a classic luncheon or supper dish. It can be a family favorite especially when you have cooked chicken or turkey on hand!

Serves: 6 to 8
Oven: 350°

Ingredients:

2 pkgs. (10 oz. ea.) frozen broccoli

2 cans (10½ oz. ea.) condensed cream of chicken soup

1 tablespoon lemon juice

1 cup mayonnaise or salad dressing

2 cups cooked chicken or turkey, sliced

½ cup grated cheese

½ cup soft bread crumbs

1 tablespoon butter or margarine, melted

Directions:

Cook broccoli until tender. Drain. Place in greased 9x13″ baking dish. Arrange chicken or turkey on top. In mixing bowl, combine soup, lemon juice and mayonnaise. Pour over chicken.

Combine cheese, bread crumbs and butter; sprinkle over casserole. Bake at 350° for 25 to 30 minutes.

Mickey Stanley

Boneless Lemon Chicken

by Dick Van Patten

Serves: 4
Oven: 350°

Chicken breasts *Italiano!* Subtle flavors of garlic, lemon, wine, and Parmesan cheese make this dish *delizioso.*

Ingredients:

4 chicken breasts, skinned boned
4 to 5 tablespoons olive oil
2 to 3 tablespoons butter
2 garlic cloves, minced
1 beaten egg, and a bit of milk

¾ cup Italian bread crumbs
2 lemons, about ½ cup of juice
½ cup white wine
Romano or Parmesan cheese, grated

Directions:

Heat oil and butter until very light, golden color. Add garlic cloves. Cook until slightly brown and remove. Chicken breasts should resemble veal cutlets.

Dip chicken pieces into egg mixture, then into crumb mixture. Gently brown in oil mixture for about 15 to 20 minutes. Salt and pepper.

Place chicken in a 9x13" dish. Pour combined lemon juice and wine over top. Sprinkle with grated cheese. Cover and bake at 350° for 30 to 40 minutes.

Dick Van Patten

Chicken Hawaiian

by Henry Winkler

Serves: 8
Oven: 325°

"The recipe has been in my family's cookbook for a long time. It has given my mouth a party for many a year. The Special Olympics give self respect and self respect is cool."

Ingredients:

2 medium fryers, cut up
¼ cup butter
2 tablespoons flour
1 cup orange juice
1 can (14½ oz.) chicken broth
1 teaspoon salt

dash of cayenne, garlic salt and cinnamon
1 can (20 oz.) pineapple chunks
½ cup raisins
2 oz. slivered blanched almonds

Directions:

Brown chicken pieces in melted butter in a large Dutch oven or heavy skillet. Remove chicken as it browns. Pour off all but 4 tablespoons fat. Stir in flour and cook and stir for 5 minutes. Gradually stir in orange juice and broth. Return chicken to Dutch oven. Add salt, cayenne, cinnamon, pineapple and juice, and raisins. Cover and simmer over low heat 50 to 60 minutes, or until chicken is tender, or bake at 325° for 1½ to 2 hours. Sprinkle with almonds. Garnish with parsley and orange slices.

SPECIAL OLYMPICS
A WAY TO LOVE

NINE

Salads

Kentucky Ambrosia Salad

by Phyllis George Brown

"Mother used to fix Ambrosia for our family in Texas. And in my new home here in Kentucky, Ambrosia is a favorite dish with dinner or afterwards as a dessert. It's yummy! The more you add the more you can serve. The coconut makes it! Use a big clear glass salad bowl."

Serves: 8 to 10

Ingredients:

1 cup Mandarin oranges, drained (tangerines can be used, too.)
1 cup pineapple tidbits, drained
3 bananas, sliced
1 cup miniature marshmallows

1 cup coconut
1 cup sour cream
1 tablespoon mayonnaise
maraschino cherries, if desired
*Any combination of fresh fruit can be used.

Directions:

Combine fruits. Mix sour cream and mayonnaise. Fold in fruit. Add coconut and marshmallows. Garnish with cherries.

Phyllis George Brown

Christmas Salad Vinaigrette

by Jo Cahow

A marvelous vegetable marinade ideal for holiday time. It can be prepared ahead of time and looks like Christmas!

Serves: 10 to 12

Ingredients:

4 cups or 2 pkgs. frozen brussel sprouts
1 cup halved cherry tomatoes
1 cup sliced raw mushrooms
1 cup vegetable oil
⅓ cup cider vinegar
1½ teaspoons sugar

1 teaspoon salt
½ teaspoon garlic salt
2 tablespoons minced green pepper
2 tablespoons minced green onion
2 tablespoons chopped parsley
4 drops Tabasco sauce

Directions:

Cook brussel sprouts. Cut in halves or quarters. Add to tomatoes and mushrooms.

Combine oil, vinegar, salt, garlic salt, onion, pepper, parsley and Tabasco sauce. Put in jar. Shake well to mix.

Pour over brussel sprout mixture. Chill. Stir occasionally. Best if made 24 hours ahead of time.

Avocado and Grapefruit Salad

by Phyllis Diller

This attractive salad is perfect for a party or family. The salad dressing is easy to prepare and delicious.

Serves: 4

SALAD

Ingredients:

1 head iceberg lettuce
1 large grapefruit, sectioned

1 avocado, cut into slices

Directions:

Make a bed of lettuce on a large flat salad plate. Alternate thin lengthwise slices of grapefruit sections and avocado.

Pour on German Dressing and salt and pepper (coarse, cracked). Serve as first course, alone, or as a main course at lunch.

GERMAN DRESSING

Ingredients:

When a bottle of catsup or preferably chili sauce has about an inch or so left in the bottom (the last is impossible to get out) *or*

2 tablespoons pour in:
1 cup oil
¼ cup apple cider vinegar
1½ tablespoons sugar

Directions:

Shake well and always shake again before serving. This dressing keeps indefinitely refrigerated.

Phyllis Diller

Ambrosia

by Rafer Johnson

This mellow blend of fruits, nuts, marshmallows and coconut are bound together with sour cream. Serve it as a salad or dessert.

Serves: 12 to 14

Ingredients:

1 can (16 oz.) crushed pineapple

3 to 4 small cans (11 oz. ea.) mandarin oranges

4 cartons (8 oz. ea.) sour cream

1 bag (10½ oz.) small marshmallows

½ cup walnuts, chopped

1 cup shredded coconut

¼ cup maraschino cherries, sliced

Directions:

Drain the pineapple and mandarin oranges. Add sour cream. Mix well. Add marshmallows, walnuts, coconut and cherries. It tastes best if you refrigerate overnight.

Caesar Salad

by Ron Kramer

Now you can enjoy a Caesar Salad at home, just like at your favorite restaurant!

Serves: 6 to 8

Dressing:

Ingredients:

¼ cup wine vinegar
¼ cup Italian olive oil
½ teaspoon dry mustard
1 teaspoon
    Worcestershire sauce
½ teaspoon garlic powder
1 can anchovies
½ lemon, squeezed
¼ teaspoon ground pepper
3 tablespoons Parmesan
    cheese

2 eggs, coddled
2 heads of romaine lettuce
    (cleaned, wrapped in
    towel and refrigerated
    for 2 hours)

Directions:

Put all ingredients (except lettuce and eggs) in blender and mix. When ingredients are sufficiently blended, pour into a very large bowl. Add eggs and mix. Break lettuce with hand, do not cut, and mix with the ingredients. Add croutons, cracked pepper and Parmesan cheese to your liking.

Ron Kramer

Hickory Hill Salad

by Ethel Kennedy

Serves: 4 to 6

There's a place in Virginia where this famous lady enter-tains and enjoys her family and friends. The Hickory Hill Salad is truly delicious and it contains a surprise use of cream cheese, cut into small cubes.

Ingredients:

1 head iceberg lettuce
¼ cup diced carrots
¼ cup diced green peppers
¼ cup cubed cream cheese
½ cup peeled halved sliced
    cucumbers
½ cup crumbled cooked
    bacon

1 avocado, peeled and
    sliced
1 small red onion, sliced and
    in rings
croutons
your favorite dressing

Directions:

In a large bowl, layer the lettuce, carrots, green peppers, cream cheese, cucumbers and bacon. Add avocado, onion and croutons, to garnish. Add dressing.

Ethel Kennedy

"THE MEASURE OF AN INDIVIDUAL'S ACHIEVEMENT IS NOT WHETHER HE WINS OR LOSES, BUT IN THE SPIRIT HE DISPLAYS ..."

Italian Salad Regis

by Mama D

Mama D. says, "I'm no Julia Child. I tell you to wash your hands and then use them. Years ago women used their hands in cooking, kneading dough. Break the lettuce with your hands, never use a knife."

Serves: 6 to 8

Ingredients:

3 tablespoons oil
1 tablespoon wine vinegar
1 head lettuce, torn into
　　pieces
6 thin slices your favorite
　　cheese, cut up
6 thin slices ham, cut up
6 thin slices roast beef,
　　cut up
1 green pepper, chopped

18 thin slices pepperoni
1 onion, finely chopped
1 clove garlic, minced
salt to taste
1 zucchini, sliced
12 green olives, sliced
$\frac{1}{8}$ teaspoon oregano
1 tablespoon Romano
　　cheese, grated
2 or 3 tomatoes, cut into
　　wedges

Directions:

Shake oil and vinegar together. Put all other ingredients except Romano cheese and tomatoes in a salad bowl and toss gently. Drizzle oil and vinegar over salad. Sprinkle with Romano cheese. Garnish with tomato wedges.

Mama D

176

Hungry Swimmer Salad

by John Naber

You don't have to be an Olympic Gold Medalist to enjoy this salad. It's delicious and nutritious!

Serves: 1 *very* hungry swimmer or 2 hungry swimmers

Ingredients:

¼ head iceberg lettuce
¼ head romaine lettuce
1 apple, diced
1 orange, diced
1 carrot, sliced
3 slices sandwich ham, sliced or shredded
3 slices Swiss cheese, sliced or shredded

1 hard cooked egg sliced
1 tablespoon sunflower seeds
1 tablespoon raisins
8 to 10 Wheat Thins crackers, crushed
1 cup Hidden Valley Ranch Style Dressing
½ cucumber, sliced

Directions:

Toss in a large bowl!

John Naber

California Salad Bowl

by Cheryl Tiegs

A refreshing salad for any meal, but special for a buffet. The mild curry dressing compliments the avocado, bacon, chicken, and blue cheese combination.

Serves: 10

Ingredients:

1½ quarts escarole or chicory lettuce, torn
1 quart iceberg lettuce, torn
½ cup sliced scallions
1 lb. bacon
1½ medium avocados

1 tablespoon lemon juice
1½ cups chopped cooked chicken
½ cup blue cheese, crumbled
¾ to 1 cup curry dressing

Directions:

Combine lettuce and scallions. Place in plastic bag and refrigerate until ready to serve. Cook bacon until very crisp. Drain and crumble. Peel avocado and remove pit. Sprinkle with lemon juice.

When ready to serve, place greens in a bowl. Dice avocado. Arrange rows of avocado, bacon, chicken and blue cheese over greens. Pour curry dressing on salad.

Curry dressing:

Yield: 1 cup

¼ cup vinegar
1 tablespoon water
⅔ cup vegetable oil

½ teaspoon salt
⅛ teaspoon sugar
¼ teaspoon curry powder

Directions:

Combine all ingredients in a covered jar and shake well. Refrigerate. Shake well just before tossing salad. Makes about 1 cup.

Cheryl Tiegs

Yogurt Fruit Salad

by Dennis Weaver

This unique salad is a lesson in nutrition and the author says,"Toss with a flare."

Serves: 4

Ingredients:

2 cups fruit yogurt, "protein, good intestinal bacteria"
1 banana, "potassium"
1 apple, "potassium"
1 peach, "vitamin C"
1 pear, "minerals"
½ cup berries, "color"
½ papaya, "digestive enzyme"
½ pineapple, "digestive enzyme"

Topping: any combination

1 teaspoon lecithin, "roto rooter for the arteries"
1 teaspoon Brewers yeast, "fantastic get up and go"
1 teaspoon pumpkin seeds, "unsaturated fatty acids"
1 teaspoon sunflower seeds, "beautiful skin"
1 teaspoon raisins, "protein"
1 teaspoon cashew nuts, "protein"

Directions:

Slice fruit in bite size pieces. Add yogurt and mix. Add topping mixture of your choice.

Dennis Weaver

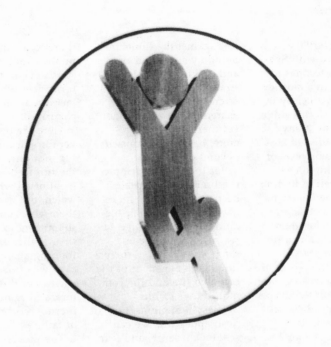

SPECIAL OLYMPICS, INC.

Eunice Kennedy Shriver, *President*
Robert M. Montague, Brig. Gen. U.S.A. (Ret.), *Executive Director*

Created and sponsored by
The Joseph P. Kennedy, Jr. Foundation

Special Olympics: What's So Special?

by Ralph B. Potter

ALMOST everyone associated with Special Olympics testifies to being moved in a most extraordinary manner by involvement with this singular sports event. Many highly accomplished athletes, veterans of years of training and high-level competition tell of finding a special revelation of the meaning of sport, an understanding richer than any they had attained in more heralded arenas. Wherein lies the power of Special Olympics to shed such light upon the deeper significance and satisfactions available in the diverse realm of sport?

The excellence and the drama which reveal the meaning of sport to those who share in Special Olympics do not rest in the exhibition of physical superiority or in the clever promotion of new variations on the theme of "the thrill of victory and the agony of defeat." The impact of Special Olympics upon us seems, rather, to reside in our capacity to identify with the competitors' striving against their limits and limitations; in our ability to apply to our own lives the example of their hope, and will, and courage to overcome.

We all have limits and limitations. World record holders represent us in the struggle of our human species against the limits imposed by space and time and gravity. They demonstrate to us what our kind of creature can do. We share in their achievement; yet their struggle is remote, beyond our capacity, beyond our need.

But in Special Olympics the limits of our species become, as it were, incarnate in the particular limitations which threaten to restrict our neighbors' range of activity, participation, and enjoyment of the common life and the common things of life.

These limitations, now in flesh appearing, we can see, touch, sense, and fear. But we can also experience a burst of delight, relief, excitement and resolve in witnessing their conquest. We can come to realize that our own secret or not so secret limitations, which we feared would bar us from fullest participation and enjoyment, can be challenged and overcome. More is possible than ever we had dared suppose.

In Special Olympics, this liberation of powers, this victory over the limitations imposed upon us by nature, by ourselves, by other persons, or by custom, takes place not simply in an interior, private, isolated world of fantasy, but in the "real world", the world of space and time, in front of all who are there to behold. It is a public event, indeed, a sports event, featuring performances which can be measured, timed, judged, compared.

Here are persons so long kept in darkness, in hiding, not only appearing in the full light of day in front of all who care to watch, but daring to "put themselves on the line" submitting to a test of their ability and level of training against the physical laws of nature, the capacities of their competitors, and against their own inertia, reticence, and fear of failure.

The power of Special Olympics as a sports event able to evoke profound reactions in the absence of physical superiority and highly publicized personal "drama", rests in its exhibition of a specific form of moral excellence, the courage to be, to be oneself, to be known to be what one is, and to aspire to become yet more. It is as a festival of liberation, hope, and courage, made visible in the simplest manner through physical contests we all can understand, against limits and limitations we all can appreciate, that Special Olympics so deeply enriches our understanding and appreciation of the human struggles that go on around us and within us, all of us, day by day.

Ralph B. Potter is Professor of Social Ethics at the Harvard Divinity School.

Special Olympics Volunteers:

250,000

"Someone Elses"

by Colman McCarthy
Washington Post

A S with most other males who were conditioned early to believe that success in sports meant playing for big money in big arenas, I learned only slowly that that was false. My teachers in the lessons of true athletics have been some mentally retarded youngsters, children who are part of the Special Olympics program.

More than any other movement in American sports in the past decade, Special Olympics has gone into communities, neighborhoods and families to spread a spirit of playfulness that is, or should be, the essential vibrancy of sports.

If the poet Wallace Stevens is right, that "we are all hot with the imperfect," then what has been happening through the Special Olympics is unique: The mentally retarded are helping the intellectually retarded.

The latter are those of us whose minds build shelves for the handicapped and then stash them away like undusted bric-a-brac to be forgotten. Or those who hire zoning lawyers to defend the purity of the neighborhood when the retarded dare move into a half-way house. Or those who read the latest newspaper expose about the filthy conditions in the state home for the retarded and murmur that "something should be done." By someone else.

One of the beauties of the Special Olympics is that it has attracted the someone elses in amazingly large numbers—the quarter of a million volunteers. Few national programs are receiving the unsalaried energies of more groups, from amateurs like the American Legion and the Road Runners Club of America to the National Basketball Association and the North American Soccer League.

As for those volunteers who do more for the retarded than any outsider can imagine—the fathers and mothers of the children—they report that Special Olympics can enhance family life in the most uplifting of ways.

I have seen this in my own neighborhood, in Angela Mann, a 15-year-old who has Down's syndrome and who won two medals in the District of Columbia Special Olympics earlier this month. Her father, Dr. Jesse Mann, a professor of philosophy at Georgetown University and the only person I know who can discuss Heidegger while mowing his lawn, tells of Angela's new sense of her abilities. Now that she has seen herself excel in the 50-yard dash, she has become open to finding more occasions to excel.

Other families around the country report the same. Special Olympics, through its teaching clinics and the Let's Play to Grow Program, is helping parents gain knowledge and confidence in working with their retarded children.

Not every retarded child is in Special Olympics and not all parents are blessed with the spiritual strength to keep nurturing their child despite the seemingly slow progress. But in only a decade, Special Olympics has become a world-class example of what can be done if a few people put their minds — and their bodies — to it.

Milestones in

1963: Kennedy Foundation and American Association for Health, Physical Education and Recreation cooperate on a physical fitness program for mentally retarded inviduals and offer awards for achievement.

July 1968: First International Special Olympics held at Chicago's Soldier Field with 1,000 participants.

December 1968: Senator Kennedy announces establishment of Special Olympics, Inc. The National Association for Retarded Citizens pledges its national support.

January 1970: All 50 states, the District of Columbia and Canada have Special Olympics organizations and State Directors. 50,000 athletes are involved.

March 1970: National Hockey League Board of Governors announces sponsorship of International Special Olympics Floor Hockey Program.

June 1970: 550 young athletes participate in the First French Special Olympics Games—the first instance of significant participation outside the U.S.

August 1970: 150,000 Special Olympians and 65,000 volunteers now involved in more than 1,400 local and area meets. All states hold State Special Olympics Games.

August 1970: Second International Special Olympics Games take place in Chicago with 2,000 athletes from 50 states, the District of Columbia, Canada, France and Puerto Rico.

December 1971: U.S. Olympic Committee gives Special Olympics official approval as one of only two organizations entitled to use name "Olympics."

June 1972: Jean Claude Killy, world champion skier, welcomes 1,500 young French athletes to French Special Olympics Games.

August 1972: Third International Games open on campus of Univervity of California at Los Angeles with 2,500 participants. Elree Bivens sets mile record of 4 minutes 48 seconds. Texas team sets 440-relay mark of 53 seconds.

April 1973: ABC television broadcasts segment covering Special Olympics on "Wide World of Sports." program.

June 1973: Pierre Mazeaud, French Minister of Youth and Sports, attends French Special Olympics Games. Spirit and courage of athletes moves him on the spot to offer six silver cups as trophies.

January 1974: More than 300,000 children now active in Special Olympics year-round, including 15,000 local meets and games.

April 1974: Kyle Rote, Jr. winner of the ABC Superstars Competition, contributes $5,000 of his prize money to Special Olympics.

June 1974: National Hockey League hosts third annual Floor Hockey Tournament in Winnipeg. Philadelphia team wins Little Stanley Cup. Team from St. Louis captures Clarence Campbell Bowl.

July 1974: 400,000 athletes take part in 1974 Special Olympics program showing that participation continues to expand.

December 1974: National Basketball Association and American Basketball Association cooperate to sponsor the National Special Olympics Basketball Program, including exciting Run, Dribble and Shoot competition.

February 1975: Winner of second Superstars Competition, O.J. Simpson, contributes $5,000 of his prize money to Special Olympics following the lead set by Kyle Rote, Jr. a year earlier.

March 1975: First Presidential Premiere for Special Olympics features Barbra Streisand and *Funny Lady*. 10 million Americans see TV Special featuring President Ford. Muhammad Ali, Frank Gifford and Special Olympics athletes.

Special Olympics

March-April 1975: 3,182 Non-commissioned officers run from Washington, D.C. and Los Angeles, California non-stop in a 3,182 mile marathon for Special Olympics. Hundreds of high school and college track and cross country teams, jogging associations, running clubs and concerned volunteers join to help raise funds to send athletes to the International Special Olympics Games.

April 1975: Mexican athletes compete for the first time in a Special Olympics in Nogales, Arizona.

August 1975: Fourth International Special Olympics Games take place with 3,200 young athletes participating from ten countries at Central Michigan University. CBS television broadcast event on "Sports Spectacular" show.

September 1975-August 1976: International expansion occurs from impetus of 1975 International Games. New programs start in Hong Kong, the Bahamas, Honduras, Okinawa and other countries.

February 1977: First International Winter Special Olympics brings over 500 athletes to Steamboat Springs, Colorado to learn to ski and skate. CBS, ABC, and NBC television all cover event.

March 1977: Grey Advertising volunteers to serve as public service advertising agency for Special Olympics internationally.

July 1977: Participation in Special Olympics climbs to over 700,000 with increased number of adult participants, 19 countries now have Special Olympics.

August 1977: Bruce Jenner, world's greatest athlete, becomes Head Coach of Special Olympics track and field activities.

September 1977: Special Olympics launches worldwide soccer program with Pelé as Head Coach and sponsorship by North American Soccer League.

November 1977: Governor Carey, Eunice Kennedy Shriver and Dr. Albert Brown announce award of Fifth International Summer Special Olympics Games in August, 1979 to the State University of New York College at Brockport.

February 1978: CBS telecasts two-hour movie "Special Olympics" in prime time telling the story of how the program affects a typical family having a mentally retarded child.

July 1978: Special Olympics games, held in each state and country each year, are featured in a half-hour NBC telecast during prime sports time on Sunday. Growth of program to 1,000,000 participants is announced.

December 1978: Second Presidential Premiere for Special Olympics held in Washington, D.C., New York, Boston and Chicago, featuring *Superman, The Movie*. Special Olympics inaugurates the "Spirit of Special Olympics" Award, presented by Mrs. Jimmy Carter to 11 Special Olympians who, both on and off the playing field, display those qualities of skill, sharing, joy and courage which are the essence of Special Olympics.

April 1979: Rocky Bleier of the Pittsburgh Steelers is first non-Special Olympian to receive the "Spirit of Special Olympics" Award.

July 1979: Special Olympics Commemorative Stamp is unveiled in ceremony at the White House. Ron Guidry of the New York Yankees receives second "Spirit of Special Olympics" Award granted to a non-Special Olympian.

August 1979: Fifth International Summer Special Olympics Games take place with 3,500 athletes participating from every state and more than 20 countries at the State University of New York College at Brockport. ABC-TV broadcasts event on "Wide World of Sports."

*"Physical activity and competitive sports are essential
companions to the qualities of intellect and spirit on which a nation is built."*
John F. Kennedy

Index

Celebrities

Index

Recipes
Alphabetical

A

B

191

C

F

H

I

L

M

P

Q

R

S

T

V

W

A Note About The Coeditors

Kathryn Buursma and Mary Stickney conceived and planned the OFFICIAL SPECIAL OLYMPICS CELEBRITY COOK BOOK. They collected and tested each of these excellent recipes. Kathy is involved with Special Education Classes in Grand Rapids, Michigan, where she developed a keen interest in the Special Olympics. She and Mary attended the 1979 Special Olympics Winter Regional Games at Schuss Mountain in upstate Michigan.

After reminiscing about Special Olympians, the idea came to them to collect favorite recipes of hundreds of well-known athletes and other celebrities who are involved with Special Olympics.

Kathryn and Mary are sisters. Each has a continuing interest in cooking and cook books because of Mom's (Esther Hall) interest and influence.

Both are married with two teenagers apiece. They and their families reside in Grand Rapids, Michigan.

Kathryn and Mary are pleased to help the Special Olympics because they care.

SPECIAL OLYMPICS